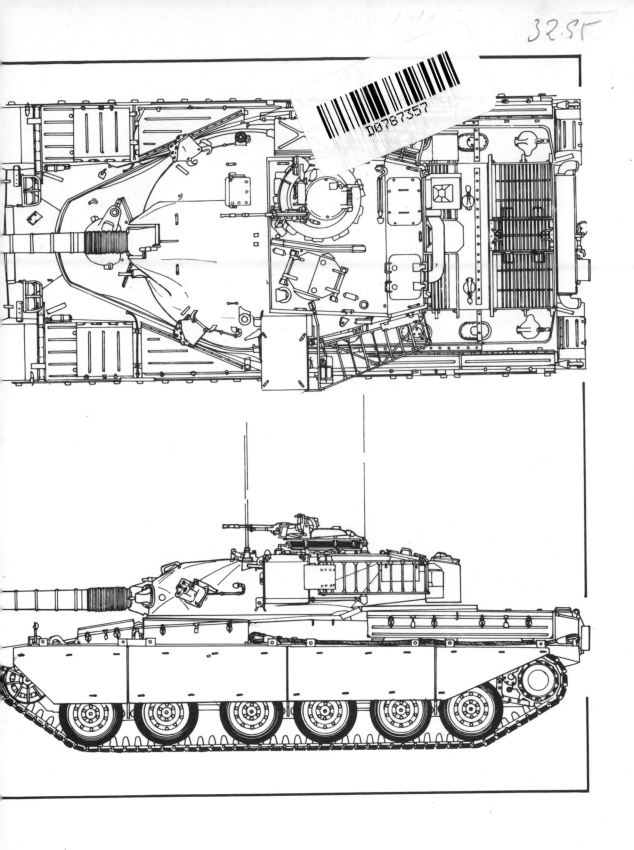

Modern Combat Vehicles:1
CHIEFTAIN

George Forty

LONDON

IAN ALLAN LTD

First published 1979

ISBN 0 7110 0943 9

Design by Anthony Wirkus LSIAD

© George Forty 1979

Published by Ian Allan Ltd, Shepperton, Surrey;
and printed in the United Kingdom by
Ian Allan Printing Ltd

Contents

Title page: Chieftains of A Squadron 4RTR in front of Berlin's Olympic Stadium during their annual 'Arras Day' parade, 1974. / *Crown copyright*

Left: Mud, glorious mud! Chieftains of 17/21 Lancers plough their way across the mud of Hohne Ranges. / *Crown copyright*

Chieftains of 4/7 Royal Dragoon Guards taking part in exercises at the British Army Training Unit, Suffield, Alberta. / *Crown copyright*

Introduction

The Chieftain has now been in service with the British Army for over a decade and will certainly stay with us for at least another 10 years. So, at somewhere around the half-way mark in its service life span, this is not a bad point at which to take stock of our current main battle tank, although it will undoubtedly have a much longer useful life elsewhere in the world just as its predecessor, the Centurion, has done. By the time that my own regiment, the 4th Royal Tank Regiment, came to be equipped with Chieftain, I was a member of Regimental Headquarters and thus more intimately concerned with the internal workings of the FV432 Command Vehicles than with the tanks. My fighting days had been spent in Centurion, and, having commanded a troop in action in Korea during the early 1950s, my affections still lay with the Cent and not with this rather awe-inspiring, streamlined monster with its enormous gun. The first time I was shown over a Chieftain I remember thinking how complicated the gun control equipment in the turret appeared, after the relatively simple gear in the Centurion. But opinions change and I had similar thoughts the first time I was introduced to the new fire control system, IFCS. No doubt future gunners and commanders will find it perfectly easy to operate and will wonder why we ever put up with anything less efficient.

Chieftain has had its share of problems, particularly on the automotive side, and I have deliberately tried not to gloss over these defects, some of which are only now being cured. However, let me say at the very beginning of this book that I consider Chieftain to be a very fine tank. Its gun and gun control equipment are superior to anything in service anywhere else in the world, and the advent of IFCS will enhance this superiority. As mobile firepower is the primary reason for having a tank in the first place, Chieftain gets full marks from me in that respect straight away.

As I have never been a very technically minded officer, it was with some trepidation that I approached the subject of describing a modern armoured fighting vehicle. Fortunately, like most of those who have been privileged to serve in Her Majesty's Forces, I have made a lot of good friends and consequently have been able to draw upon their expertise to get me out of difficulties. The opening chapter in the book is written by one of our most knowledgeable tank designers, Leslie Monger, MBE, who has now retired from the Military Vehicles and Engineering Establishment (MVEE) after 35 years of service devoted to AFV design and development. He played a major part in designing Chieftain, so it was the greatest good fortune that I was able to persuade him to assist me. He has produced a fascinating account of how Chieftain's configuration was decided and its main components selected and I am eternally grateful to him for his help. I have also had magnificent assistance from the many firms in this country which make components for Chieftain, the list of acknowledgements is a long one and does, I hope, reflect the great good will of all these splendid firms. Following Les Monger's opening narrative, I have tried to trace the difficult trials period, highlighting it with eye-witness accounts of those who actually did the work. This is followed by a chapter about early 'in-service' days of Chieftain with the Eleventh Hussars, the first regiment to be completely equipped with the new tank. The 'Cherry Pickers' were a very fine regiment and their high reputation is continued by their successors, the Royal Hussars. This chapter is followed by a detailed description of the AFV and of its primary characteristics. Next follows some down-to-earth accounts of soldiering in a Chieftain tank written mainly by members of my old regiment. I hope that they will bring suitably nostalgic whiffs of cordite and diesel oil, to those who haven't been inside a tank for a while, and who, like me, can never forget the deep bond of affection that binds a 'tankie' to his beloved metal monster.

Although Chieftain has been mentioned in many books about tanks, I think this is the first time that anyone has attempted to write a complete book about this remarkable vehicle. It has been a stimulating experience for me and I hope the result will appeal to an ever growing number of tank enthusiasts.

Bradford, 1978   *George Forty*

5

Acknowledgements

I would like to thank the following for their help and advice during the preparation of this book and for providing the marvellous photographs:

Government Departments, Service Establishments and Units
MOD Directorate of Public Relations: PR HQ BAOR; PR HQ UKLF; PR HQ 1 (BR) Corps; PR Berlin; PR HQ 1st, 2nd, 3rd and 4th Divs; MVEE Chertsey; RARDE; HQ and all Schools RAC Centre; TD & PW RAC Centre; HQ Royal Ordnance Factories; ROF Leeds; ROF Blackburn; RSAF Enfield; Dept of Photographs Imperial War Museum; Photo Library Central Office of Information; Editor *Joint Services Recognition Journal*; Editor *Soldier*; Tank Museum; SEME Borden; 18 Comd Wksp REME; RHQ RSDG; RHQ RH and Home HQ RH; RHQ RTR and RTR Publications; RHQ 1, 2, 3 and 4 RTR.

Civilian Firms
Associated Press Ltd; Colour Library Daily Telegraph; Barr & Stroud Ltd; S. G. Brown Communications Ltd; Driclad Ltd; FPT Industries Ltd; Marconi Radar Systems Ltd; Marconi Space and Defence Systems Ltd (including the Military Data and the Military Communications Divisions of MSDS); ITT Components Group Europe; MEL Equipment Co Ltd; Morfax Ltd; Pilkington PE Ltd; The Plessey Co Ltd; Racal Amplivox Communications Ltd; Rolls-Royce Motors Military Engine Division: Solartron Electronic Group Ltd; Vickers Ltd; Wharton Engineers (Elstree) Ltd; and Scammell Motors.

Individuals
Maj T. B. Andrews, MBE, 9/12 L; Maj A. A. Cornish, BEM, RTR; Maj K. C. Dudley Retd; E. Flatters, Esq; WO2 B. Gormley, BEM, RH; Maj C. H. Gray, Retd; Capt J. C. W. Gillman, 15/19 H; Lt-Col A. E. Hay, Retd; Capt B. H. Hayward-Cripps, RTR; Col P. M. Hamer, OBE, Retd; Lt-Col D. R. Ivy, RTR; J. Lewis, Esq; L. Monger, Esq, MBE; Lt-Col M.W. Newcombe, GM, Retd; Tpr E. Reid, RTR; Cpl A. Smee, RTR; Capt M. N. E. Speller, RTR; and Capt R. P. C. Vaux, RTR.

A special thanks must go to K. Jones who supplied the Chieftain Mk 3 endpapers and to P. Winding for all the other excellent line drawings.

1. Birth of a Tank

As I have already explained in the Introduction, I have been fortunate enough to persuade Leslie Monger to write this all important first chapter in which he explains the reasoning behind the selected configuration of the Chieftain tank. Les spent his early years in the commercial vehicle industry, starting off with J. I. Thornycroft and later was with Leyland Motors. He joined the Department of Tank Design in 1941 and until 1943 was engaged in trying to correct some of the weaknesses of our wartime tanks — Crusader, Covenanter, Centaur and Cromwell. Late in 1943, he joined the team engaged on the design and development of Centurion. In 1948 he became the first member of a new group specialising in the concept design of all types of armoured fighting vehicles. He continued as the principal engineer of the group for over 24 years, and in this capacity did much pioneering work on the derivatives of Centurion, the FV430 family, Anti-tank Guided Missile Launchers, Chieftain, the Light Tracked Vehicle CVR(T) and the Future Main Battle Tank which will eventually replace Chieftain. The group also designed training aids and assessed foreign AFVs. From 1972 to 1976 he was the Secretary of both the Concepts Design Group and the Technical Control Committee for the Joint UK/FRG studies of the Future Main Battle Tank. He was awarded the MBE in 1975 and has now retired from MVEE and lives in Camberley. The Army, and in particular the Royal Armoured Corps, owes a great deal to men like Les, who have devoted their lives to designing our vehicles, and he is clearly the best possible person to explain the evolution of Chieftain.

The Design Aim

Chieftain was intended to replace the Medium Tank Centurion and it was known during the early stages of design as Medium Tank No 2. Later it took on the role of a Main Battle Tank for reasons which will be explained as the story unfolds.

When the studies were started in 1950 Centurion had already established itself worldwide as a successful tank, but its superiority over its adversaries could not last indefinitely and it was judged that its phasing out would have to start in the 1960s. Its replacement would then have to remain in service until the 1980s, so it had to be able to defeat the best that any potential enemy could put on the battefield in that era.

The weapon carried by Centurion's successor not only had to ensure defeat of the future target but it had to do it at longer range and more quickly to counteract the superiority in enemy numbers which was anticipated.

Protection was needed to withstand the threat of the anti-tank weapons of the future which were expected to be a mixture of kinetic and chemical energy attack. The latter was expected to be hollow charge from guns and guided missiles. Improved mobility was needed but this was not easy to define because, unlike the weapon and protection performances, it could not be stated in finite values which were critical for success in battle. Improved agility was needed rather than speed.

From the start of the studies there was no doubt that the new tank could have the necessary improved firepower and protection against kinetic energy attack. There was hope that a measure of protection would be possible against hollow charge attack, but as that threat was still being developed there was less certainty about the degree of protection which would be possible.

Already the development of Centurion's supporting heavy tank, Conqueror, had shown that the weapon system and armour envisaged for the Medium Tank No 2 could, in a conventional design of tank, increase the weight from Centurion's 52.9 tonnes (52 tons) to 66 tonnes (65 tons). Such a weight would have precluded any improvement in agility and made movement to the battlefield more difficult. Consequently the primary aim of the studies was to find a solution which would achieve the performance without the weight penalty.

The aim led to the study of unconventional designs under a Concept Study Programme the results of which are described in the following pages.

7

Concept Research Studies

Those engaged in the search for a design to succeed Centurion had to examine all possibilities and report their findings to the user who would eventually have to select the concept to be developed and produced. It would not be the ideal tank but it had to be the best compromise of firepower, protection and mobility possible with current technology. Due regard had to be taken of many other factors such as initial and in-service costs, maintainability, transportability, crew training and the overall effect on army manpower.

While the unconventional concepts were being studied it was kept in mind that the conventional tank layout had been proved in battle and might still prove to be the best solution, so means of improving it and reducing its weight were studied in parallel with the concept research work.

Alternatives to the High Velocity (HV) Gun

The size and weight of a tank is largely dependent on the size and, to a lesser extent, the weight of its weapon system including ammunition, always assuming that it has sufficient mobility to get to its battle station and protection enough to survive there to do its job. The possibilities of saving weight by installing alternative weapons to the high velocity gun were examined as described in the following examples.

Anti-tank Guided Missile

These were examined as primary tank weapons with machine guns as auxiliary weapons. The fighting compartment of the most promising of the guided missile launcher concepts was simulated in a rig. It was made as a wheeled trailer so that it could be sent by air to Australia for trials with the Malkara missile which had been designed there. With missiles and crew under heavy armour the problem of getting the missile to its outside launch position led to large and heavy concepts. Lighter concepts carrying missiles outside ready to launch, were drawn but were too vulnerable to all forms of enemy attack to survive in the role of a tank. As well as being too heavy, the missile launcher was tactically inferior to the gun tank. It was unsuitable for HE fire and was much less effective against multiple targets. It was better at extreme ranges but its short range capability was poor. The guided missile could deliver only a chemical energy warhead, so an enemy could protect himself against it more easily than if he had to face the HV gun firing kinetic and chemical energy protectiles.

Guided Missiles plus a Low Velocity Gun or Free Flight Rockets

Attempts were made to overcome the tactical disadvantage of the guided missile against targets which required HE fire, by using a dual weapon system. In some concepts, guided missiles and a low

Left: Model of rig simulating the fighting compartment of an armoured launcher for the anti-tank missile Malkara. / *Crown copyright*

Right: Sheridan with tube-launched anti-tank missile system Shillelagh. / *Crown copyright*

velocity gun were installed, in others free flight rockets were used to support the guided missiles. The tactical weaknesses against multiple and short range armour targets remained and the concepts were excessively large and heavy or too lightly armoured to survive in the role of a tank. The possibility was considered that a lightly armoured missile launcher might survive by using its ability to engage tank targets without the direct line needed between the gun and target. Remote vision and guidance was feasible to permit the launcher to remain behind cover whilst engaging its target. A launcher thus equipped would have severe tactical limitations. It would be all right in a static defensive position but would be of little use for close fighting if an enemy had penetrated the defence line and it would be unable to move in the open to retake lost ground.

The Tube-Launched Missile as a Tank Weapon

At the time of the UK studies the US were already developing a tube-launched missile system which could also fire a high explosive shell. The system, known as 'Shillelagh' has since been put into service by the US in their Sheridan light tank and as an alternative to the 105mm HV gun in a proportion of their main combat tanks. Shillelagh was seriously examined as the weapon system for the UK future tank. It solved the problem of getting the missile through the armour to its launch position and it provided HE fire, although the shell was larger than the UK would have chosen. The tube calibre had to be 152mm to accept an anti-tank missile with an effective warhead. The UK would like to have advanced the process of using common weapons within NATO by accepting Shillelagh but a thorough examination failed to show that it had sufficient advantages to outweigh its disadvantages when compared with the HV gun as a tank armament. It did not make the tank lighter; it was more expensive; it was tactically less flexible because it was less effective against multiple targets and it could not be used, like the gun, with night sights. There was doubt about its guidance performance against an enemy approaching out of the sun at first or last light. Like all missile systems at that time it could not deliver a kinetic energy attack.

In later years some of the system's disadvantages were to be overcome, but when the UK had to select the weapon for their future tank the gun had so many attractions.

Concepts based on a Pair of Complementary Vehicles

Having failed to find a single vehicle concept to meet the primary aim of reducing weight, the next configuration to be examined was based on dividing the functions of the single multi-role tank between two smaller vehicles. Several different complementary weapons were studied. In the most favoured combination, one vehicle mounted an HV gun of

sufficient calibre (90mm) to defeat tank targets out to about 1,200m and to provide HE fire. The complementary vehicle carried guided missiles for use against long-range targets. The HV gun vehicle had to be heavily armoured but the other could be given less armour. The idea of replacing Centurion with two smaller vehicles was attractive to the designers but presented unacceptable logistic difficulties to the user. A pair of vehicles with one carrying an expensive missile system would have cost twice as much as a single conventional HV gun tank and the total crew would have been at least five, probably six. The maintenance load was doubled and twice as many transporters were required.

Against these disadvantages the complementary vehicles offered better agility than the single multi-role tank, particularly so because the lighter vehicles could have a track ground pressure of 0.56kg/sq cm (8lb/sq in) instead of 0.84kg/sq cm (12lb/sq in) which seemed inevitable with a single heavier vehicle. Their ability to cross lighter bridges would have been useful. The inherent weakness of the two vehicle concept which led to its rejection was tactical inflexibility for there would often be theatre conditions which suited only one of the pair. So even if the additional cost and extra men could be found, a given number of vehicle pairs would generally be less useful than the same number of single, heavier tanks.

Coupled Vehicles

The purpose of the coupled vehicle was to permit the conventional HV gun to be carried without loss of protection and with far greater agility. The coupled vehicle concept was not new; it had been used for transporting men and supplies over extreme terrain and had been studied in the US as a possible future tank design where it was known as the 'Hen and

Above: Volvo high mobility coupled vehicle. / *Crown copyright*

Chick' concept. The accompanying photograph shows a tracked coupled vehicle used by the British Army to fulfil NATO commitments in the most northern areas.

In the tank concept, one unit was automotive and the other carried the fighting equipment and crew. It could be likened to a close-coupled prime mover and trailer with all four tracks driven. There was no doubt that it offered a significant improvement in battlefield mobility but there was little evidence to show that this would be of enough use to justify the inevitable high cost and complexity. Coupled vehicles did not suffer from the tactical inflexibility of the complementary vehicles nor did they need an increase in crew numbers but the concept did present transporter problems. Its effect on the maintenance services would have depended on the time and money spent on its development and some thought that a replacement automotive unit would have been an advantage. Unless the gun was mounted high, all-round fire would not be as good as for a conventional tank. The total weight was greater than a single, conventional tank but it was planned to lessen this disadvantage by giving full protection to the fighting unit in which all the crew would ride and lighter protection for the automotive unit. The concept had its good features, but its high cost and technical development risk could only be justified if the parallel study of the more conventional single vehicle failed to produce an acceptable design.

The One and Two-Man Tank Concepts

Considerable research effort went into the study of one-man and two-man tank designs which had the

attraction of being airportable when, in the early 1950s, the UK still had worldwide commitments. The advocates at first claimed that the four crewmen of a 50 or 60 tonne tank would be more effective if each operated a one-man tank of 15 tonnes, but as studies progressed it became clear that a minimum of two men were needed to operate such vehicles. So the weight increased and the arguments in its favour were weakened. In World War II four of our lighter tanks such as the Cromwell, by attacking from all sides, could defeat a Tiger tank of greater weight, but then it was from necessity not choice and we accepted the loss of several tanks for one of the enemy. Assuming optimistically that we could, by opting for a two-man 25 tonne tank, have twice as many as if we chose a conventional four-man tank, we would *still* find that our tanks had to face superior numbers.

The weapon most suited to the two-man 25 tonne tank consisted of a pair of recoilless guns each externally mounted and fed from rotating magazines. Accepting that we should be outnumbered there seemed to be an irrefutable case for our future tank to have a weapon system superior to that of the enemy so that with modern technology he could be hit and defeated at long range. At the same time it was essential to have the ability to hit quickly at successive targets when fighting in close country. Only the conventional HV gun could provide these characteristics and only the more conventional tank could carry it and provide a satisfactory firing platform.

The Fixed Gun Concept

The configuration which has been developed by Sweden as the S Tank was also studied by the UK as a basis for a possible Medium Tank No 2. It is possible that the idea came from a French light vehicle VP90

Above: Fixed gun Swedish S Tank. / *Crown copyright*

which had been demonstrated in the UK before the tilting suspension experimental vehicle was made. Trials showed that a gun fixed in the hull could be layed in elevation with sufficient accuracy by tilting the vehicle on its suspension and although the experimental vehicle did not have the modified steering proposed for it, there was general acceptance of the feasibility of laying in azimuth by rotating the whole vehicle on its tracks. Having established that the fixed gun could be accurately layed it still remained to establish that the advantages of the concept were sufficient to outweigh its disadvantages.

A tank constructed as one armoured box would certainly weigh less than a conventional one made of two boxes, ie a hull and turret, and weight saving was the primary aim of the studies. The fixed gun can be mounted lower because its barrel does not have to depress over the hull and tracks and its breech does not have to be kept clear of the roof at depression. So further weight saving results from a lower vehicle. Without the restrictions of a turret ring a much more useful fighting space is possible. Automatic loading of the gun which had before been judged impractical became possible with a breech which did not move relative to the block of ammunition which had to be fed in to it. Consequently, a reduction in crew seemed possible. The foregoing advantages of the concept, for a while, seemed to blind its advocates to its serious disadvantages.

It is inherent in the design of a tilting suspension tank that the range of elevation and depression is related to the length of track on the ground. If a conventional length of ground contact is provided on a

11

tilting tank, the total range can be as low as six degrees which would make the tank unfightable. The short ground contact needed for an acceptable range of elevation is, however, incompatible with a high road speed or a good fast ride over rough ground. To this serious disadvantage must be added the tactical shortcomings of being unable to fire on the move or even lay before halting. Almost 20 years later, in 1975/76, experiments have shown that swing-through firing permits a measure of firing on the move but this has not been enough to make the fixed gun/turretless tank as attractive as one with a turret. Sweden found the S Tank acceptable but the UK in their successor to Centurion needed a heavier weapon and a better automotive performance and these improvements were not possible on the short ground contact inherent with the tilting suspension.

Novel Features Aimed at Weightsaving

As the studies of unconventional concepts did not bring to light any promising designs, a search was made for design changes which could be applied to otherwise conventional HV gun tank concepts. The objective in all cases was to achieve improvements in firepower, protection and mobility without the weight penalty which would have to be paid for such improvements in a more straightforward evolution of Centurion.

The External Gun Concept

Figure 1 shows an externally mounted gun in a cleft turret concept. The crew are in the same positions as in Centurion but instead of the gun moving in elevation between them, it is mounted outside in a tunnel or cleft in the turret casting. In the design drawn, the ammunition was loaded manually through an opening at the rear of the turret on to the tray of a mechanism which fed it into the gun chamber. The gun no longer had to recoil within the confines of the turret ring so it could be moved back to suit turret balance and it thus overcame the problem of the front-heavy turret associated with the advent of heavier frontal armour and gun. The crew no longer had the inconvenience of hot used cartridge cases and gun fumes in their compartment. Although the gun could be moved further back, it had to be mounted higher because the breech and loading mechanism had to clear the engine compartment when the gun was elevated. Like many other novel designs the cleft turret had attractions but it failed to contribute to the primary aim of weight saving because the irregular contour of the turret casting made it inherently heavy.

The Oscillating Turret

Whilst the UK concept research studies were progressing there was a useful interchange of ideas with the US and a number of their unusual turret

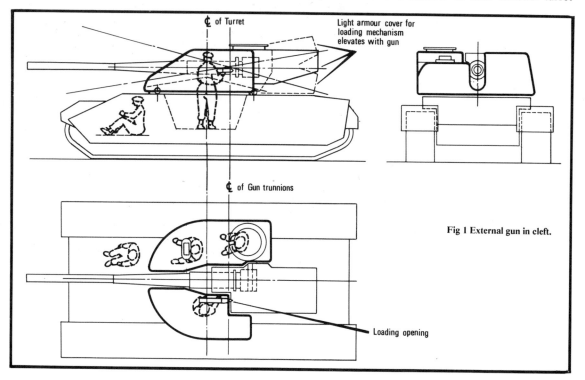

Fig 1 External gun in cleft.

configurations were the subject of drawing board studies in the UK. The one which attracted most attention was the oscillating turret concept. Here the gun was mounted integral with the turret which was mounted on a conventional turret ring. This arrangement enabled the gun to be mounted further back because it did not have to be balanced as a separate entity but as a much heavier mass. This eased the problem of turret balance. By attaching the gun and its sight to the same rigid elevating mass, troublesome linkages were avoided. The concept lent itself to the use of an auto-loader, so it might have contributed to a reduction of crew.

Despite its apparent advantages, however, the concept suffered from unacceptable disadvantages. Its overlapping armour added weight and encroached much too far into the fighting compartment. The French used an oscillating turret successfully on their AMX 10 but that had only light protection so the weight and space of its overlapping armour could be tolerated.

Auto-loaders

Reducing the volume under armour had always been an effective means of saving weight so the case for reducing volume by replacing one of the crew by an automatic loader had to be examined. Before considering if the other duties of the loader could be shared by the remaining crew, it had first to be established that a satisfactory and lighter tank could be designed with an auto-loader. It was not expected that overall manpower would be less if the tank crew was reduced because additional complexity would increase the maintenance load, but there was a strong moral case for not putting more men in the tank to be shot at than were absolutely necessary for its effective operation. A man could pick up the type of ammunition required from where it was stowed and load it into the chamber when the gun was at any elevation and azimuth angle. He could load satisfactorily when the gun was moving relative to the ammunition during a cross-country run with the gun stabilised on the target. When there was a lull in the battle he could dispose of the spent cartridge cases, which had been collected, by throwing them out of the turret. The ideal auto-loader had to do all that the man could do but some relaxations were considered.

Prototypes were made of the most promising auto-loader designs. In the design which came nearest to the ideal, a rack of ammunition was mounted on the turntable beside the gun. A swinging arm, pivoted from the gun support trunnion, collected a round, selected from the two types in the rack, and carried it to the breech where it remained on its tray following the gun movement until the round in the gun had been fired and the next was required. The number of rounds in the rack was limited. After all had been fired, or at a convenient time earlier, one of the crew had to leave his station and refill from the replenishment rounds carried elsewhere under armour. At the same time he could dispose of the spent cases.

The other prototype auto-loader was based on a type of belt mechanism which could have been mounted beside the gun or behind it in the turret bustle. The gun had to be brought back to a set angle of elevation before the selected round could be fed from the belt into the chamber. It was judged practical to bring the gun back to its loading angle and return it to its lay on target automatically but no work was done to prove the speed and accuracy of this important feature of the design.

Neither design made a significant difference to the weight of the tank and they introduced problems, especially in the troop and squadron command tanks, where the loss of a man would have most affected operational efficiency. If the design of the four-man tank, which was proceeding in parallel with the research studies, had not shown so much promise, the auto-loader concept might have been developed further.

The Liquid Propellant Gun

As the weapon performance had to be stepped-up to ensure defeat of the enemy armour, the size of the charge required to propel the HV projectile introduced difficulties. More space was needed to stow it and to move it from its stowed position to the gun and more space was needed behind the gun to load it which in turn pushed the gun trunnions forward. This, together with the increased weight of the gun and frontal armour, made it difficult to achieve the turret balance needed for a good stabilised gun control system. If the propellant could be carried in tanks and piped into the gun, only enough space would be needed behind it for recoil and to load the projectile, which two lengths are about the same. The propellant tanks could be tucked into spaces which were unsuitable for conventional charges. It was also expected that an auto-loader would be a more attractive proposition if it had only the projectile to feed into the gun. For all these reasons it was hoped that the liquid propellant would result in a lighter tank. A major difference between the cordite filled cartridge and the liquid propellant was that the former could be inserted as one piece into the chamber and ignited as soon as the breech was closed, but the liquid could not be ignited as a solid mass. Consequently the liquid was ignited as it was sprayed into the chamber. When burning started the chamber pressure began to build up and the following liquid had to be injected against a continuously increasing pressure. A gun was made and it was proved that the system could be made to work, but as the injection pump had to

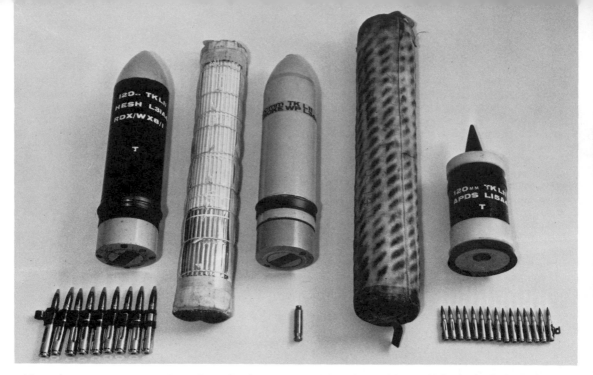

withstand pressures greater than those in the gun chamber, the size resulted in a gun in-board mass which no tank could accommodate. So what had started with so much enthusiasm failed entirely.

The Bagged Charge System

The failure of the liquid propellant project served to generate thought about other means of reducing ammunition size and from this the bagged charge concept emerged as a likely means of saving space. It was the custom for tanks to carry kinetic energy (KE) anti-armour projectiles and HE or chemical energy projectiles in the proportion 20/40. With metal cartridge cases there were cogent reasons for the same size of case to be used for all natures of ammunition, so the case size had to suit the full charge of the KE round and the HE case was only half full. With the bagged charges the total volume of cartridges was reduced by having 20 for KE at full diameter and 40 for HE at half diameter. Thus the space of 20 charges was saved in the tank. The weight of the metal cases was also saved and the space needed to collect spent cases was saved. The troublesome gun fumes, brought into the crew compartment by the ejected cases, were eliminated. The ease with which the bagged charge could be withdrawn from its stowed position enabled charges to be stowed in spaces which could not be used for metal cased ammunition.

The idea of using charges without a metal case was not new but its application to the tank was novel. The pivoted interrupted-thread breech-sealing plug, usually associated with bagged charges in artillery weapons, could not be used for rapid fire in the limited space of a tank. Without the metal case, an alternative method was needed for sealing the sliding breech block of the tank gun. A metal ring, expanded by the gas pressure in the chamber was chosen. An experimental gun was made and proved that the system was feasible. Some were worried that the bagged charge would increase the already serious ammunition fire risk so firing trials were held to allay their fears. When metal cased charges were hit they usually disrupted on impact. This was attributed to a rapid rise of pressure when the hot projectile or fragment reached the cordite. When bagged charges were struck, delays of several seconds were often noted whilst the cordite smoked before igniting; so experiments were made to see if fires could be prevented by water cooling the cordite during the delay period. Initial success with a cumbersome arrangement of water sprays led to the design of a water jacket which was more practical for installing in the tank. It needed no fire detection signal to initiate it and it released the cooling water only where it was needed, behind the projectile as it entered the cordite. The water jacket has been developed and is an important feature of Chieftain. So the bagged charge, which at first was thought by some to be a fire hazard, has given the UK tank a better protection against ammunition fires than others which still use metal cases. Trials have shown that the water jacket does not work with metal cased ammunition. Although much has been said of the reduced fire hazard, the greatest benefit of the bagged charge system is the space it saves in the tank.

Far left: Chieftain ammunition. Top row l to r: HESH anti-armour and HE projectile; bagged charge for HESH with part of the bag cut away to show sticks of cordite; smoke projectile; bagged charge for APDS; APDS projectile. Bottom row l to r: 12.7mm (0.50in) belt for Ranging Machine Gun; firing tube for 120mm gun; 7.62mm belt for coax and commander's GPMGs. / *Crown copyright*

Left: Water-jacketed bagged charge container. / *Crown copyright*

Below: Early model of Chieftain. / *Crown copyright*

THE SELECTED CONFIGURATION

Defence spending in a country as small as the UK does not allow development of alternatives, attractive as it may seem to develop a very advanced design which, if successful, would be ahead of all competitors, while at the same time developing an evolutionary design with less technical risk, so that the choice for production could be made after trials of each. Consequently, all data available from the research studies, together with all that could be found out about development in other countries, including those which could be considered potential enemies, was carefully examined to ensure that the best overall concept and the best balance of characteristics would be selected. Evaluation of the data left no doubt that the next UK tank should be an evolutionary one designed to carry an HV gun with a bagged charge ammunition system. The photograph of an early model shows the configuration selected. It was conventional in that its HV gun was mounted in an unlimited traverse turret, its crew were commander, gunner and loader in the turret, with the driver in the hull, and the engine and drive were at the rear. The major components were new and are described later. The choice of a bagged charge gun made a reduction in the overall size of the tank possible because less space was needed to stow ammunition and load it into the gun.

Reductions in height, length and width were considered as means of making volume reduction. Width could not be reduced because a wide hull was needed to support the large turret ring which would permit better sloped front armour and a balanced

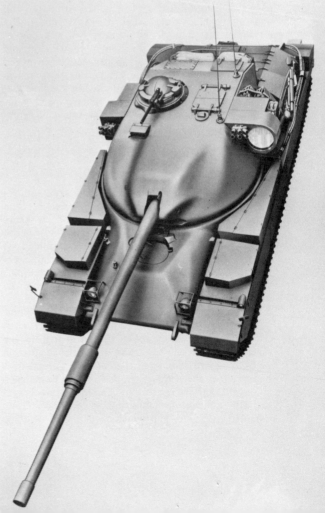

turret in spite of the heavy gun and frontal armour. Length reductions do not lead to much weight saving but height reductions make big savings because they affect the frontal armour slopes and area and, if the height reduction can be made in the hull, its heavy front, long sides and rear armour are all reduced. So means of lowering the hull had to be found. Hull heights had always been dictated by the seated driver at the front and the engine at the rear. The driver might have been taken out of the hull and put in the turret but this would have adversely influenced the layout of the turret which, it must always be remembered, is the reason for having the tank, so no loss of effectiveness was acceptable there. By reclining the driver, when in the closed-down position under armour, the hull height was reduced enough to adjust the volume to take full advantage of the bagged charge ammunition. A Centurion was modified to make a test vehicle for developing the reclining driver position and the optimum angle for his body was thus established. The engine compartment height was set to permit the gun to traverse over it at zero elevation.

In 1954 a vehicle design was selected to permit the study and development of its major components to go ahead. It incorporated a 105mm bagged charge gun and a reclining driver and it was optimistically estimated that it could be developed at a weight of 45.8 tonnes (45 tons). In the paragraphs which follow it will be seen that further improvements were judged to be so important that the weight was permitted to increase to nearly 51 tonnes (50 tons) by the time that the prototype Chieftains were running, and how, during its development, it reached a weight of nearly 55 tonnes (54 tons).

SELECTION OF THE MAJOR COMPONENTS

The Main Armament

The choice of the vehicle configuration had determined the type of main armament as a high velocity gun using bagged charge ammunition and a semi-automatic sliding breech block. The performance required from the gun, as always, determined its important design parameters, especially its calibre. Up to this stage it had been envisaged that Centurion's successor would be a Medium Tank which would, like its predecessors, be supported by a Heavy Gun Tank for engaging the heaviest armour and long-range targets. The UK and her allies had reached agreement on the targets which could be anticipated in the timescale of the new tank and had specified them in terms of a *Medium Tank Target* to be defeated at battle ranges and a *Heavy Tank Target* to be defeated at longer ranges, ie beyond 2,000m. In the early stages the UK concept for the supporting Heavy Tank mounted a 185mm gun which fired a shell weighing

about 91kg (200lb) and needed two men to load it into the breech.

It is doubtful whether a tank with this gun could ever have been put into service, but the problem was eliminated when gun and vehicle designers working together found that a 120mm HV bagged charge gun could be developed to defeat both *Medium and Heavy Tank Targets* and that it was feasible to install it in place of the 105mm gun of the selected tank configuration. *The Medium Target* could be defeated by the 120mm KE or CE projectiles and the *Heavy Tank Target* by the 120mm CE Squash Head shell which was not degraded by range. The penalty of about a tonne weight and a reduction of stowed ammunition to 53 rounds was judged to be a very acceptable price to pay for the benefits of a single tank to replace both Medium and Heavy Tanks. Chieftain, which until then had been called Medium Tank No 2, was renamed the Main Battle Tank.

A tubular primer like the one attached to the base of metal cartridge cases could not be used with a bagged charge and electrical ignition was not practical, so a gunpowder primer was sewn to the end of the charge bag and ignited by a firing tube similar in appearance to a 7.62mm cartridge. The automatic feed for the firing tubes accepted 10-round magazines. Two unusual features enhanced gun accuracy. One was an insulating jacket around the gun barrel to prevent barrel bend which could be caused when a crosswind cooled one side or rain cooled the upper side only. The other was the 12.7mm (.50in) machine gun mounted with the main armament for indicating range. The ranging machine gun (RMG) is considered later as part of the fire control system.

Target Acquisition

Having provided a long-range gun it was important to provide means of finding and identifying targets at all ranges which daylight visibility would permit and furthermore to enable targets to be acquired at night within the range of the infra-red (IR) vision devices then being developed. The commander is primarily responsible for surveillance and he is the one who must first find the target, so he was given all-round vision which he could use without opening his armoured hatch. In the centre of his frontal field of vision was a binocular periscope with both unit power and ×10 magnification, which he could use over a 360° field by rotating his cupola. For night operations he could replace the periscope with an IR instrument. When the commander had acquired the target the gunner could traverse and elevate the gun towards it and as soon as his sight was in the target area a graticule was injected into the commander's sight; thus ensuring quick and accurate opening fire. When the commander considered it more convenient he could use his overriding controls to make the final lay and fire. The range at which the IR sight could be used was enhanced by IR illumination of the target from a searchlight mounted in an armoured box on the left side of the turret. The same searchlight could also provide white light when required. The Army accepted a weight penalty of one tonne for the benefits of the searchlight. Some years later, a fully passive image intensification sight was developed to replace Chieftain's IR sight and the searchlight is not expected to be seen on later marks.

Fire Control

The gunner's periscopic sight followed the successful Centurion sight by providing ×8 monocular magnification in a unit power window. It was integral with the gun in azimuth and followed the gun in elevation, via a temperature compensated linkage. An optical link was used to inject the gunner's ballistic graticule into the commander's sight. A 12.7mm (.50in) machine gun was mounted parallel with the main gun to establish range ballistically and to aid the lay when firing the lower velocity HESH ammunition against armour targets, especially when crosswinds could affect it. Centurion practice was also followed by providing a straight-through telescope which could be used by the gunner if his periscopic sight or its linkage had been damaged. A laser rangefinder has since been developed and can be fitted retrospectively to all Chieftains. It is expected that the RMG will be omitted from later marks. Gun control systems were studied, including the hydraulic equipment favoured by the US. An electro-mechanical system was selected which was an improved form of the well tried Centurion equipment. It provided stabilisation for the turret in azimuth and for the gun in elevation.

Powerplant

The Meteor gasolene engine in Centurion had, during its early life, been prone to trouble, but during more than 15 years in tanks it had been developed to a good stage of reliability and life. Consequently, it was judged suitable for the selected MBT concept, whilst the latter, at 45 tonnes, was seven tonnes lighter than Centurion. As the new concept weight increased, however, the power of the Meteor engine became insufficient. The need for a new engine presented an opportunity to change to diesel. No suitable UK diesel was available and reliance on a foreign engine had serious risks, so it was decided that a new engine would be developed. By the end of 1957 much emphasis was being given to the new multi-fuel policy which required fighting vehicles to be able to run on a range of fuels including both gasoline and diesel. This, together with other factors, such as compactness, led to the choice in mid-1958 of an opposed-piston two-stroke compression ignition engine as the type to be developed.

Because of this choice a new and unusual design of engine had to be developed in such a short time that very little test-bed running was possible before engines were installed in prototype vehicles, the first of which was delivered by the contractor in late 1959. Concurrently, development was undertaken of a similar type of engine for the auxiliary generator. Engine replacement had been a lengthy task in Centurion, so much effort was applied to the development of a powerplant pack which could be changed more easily. The opposed piston engine, known as the L60, lent itself to the design of a pack which could be lifted out of the tank complete with its cooling system and other auxiliaries so that it could be run outside the vehicle for test purposes.

Right: Sectioned L60 opposed piston engine, showing blower and gears coupling the two crankshafts.
/ *Crown copyright*

Transmission

The transmission in Centurion had been developed over a long period by strengthening a design originally made for vehicles weighing nearer to 30 tonnes than 50. It was an efficient system, ie the loss of power in the gearbox was low, but it was not easy to use, so it presented a training problem and contributed to driver fatigue. These factors led to the selection of a design of transmission for Chieftain which was still a mechanical geared system but fully epicyclic, and still with a differential regenerative steering. The epicyclic gearing, in conjunction with a new centrifugal clutch, made it possible to provide an electrically operated gear shift to reduce driver training and fatigue.

Suspension

Three types of suspension emerged from the studies as possible for the new tank. A hydro-gas system with its high wheel lift and controlled spring rate would provide a good ride, torsion bars with such innovations as tube over bar which increased the effective length of the bar, would also provide a high wheel lift and comfortable ride and a Horstmann type system with coil spring packs evolved from Centurion would provide a known acceptable ride and avoid development risks. The hydro-gas system was complex, its cost was high and it entailed a risk of reliability and maintenance problems. The torsion bars increased vehicle height and were difficult to replace after mine damage. An improved version of the Centurion system was selected. It is shown in Fig 2.

Tracks

Track design had to be a compromise between the characteristics needed for performance, life, cost and

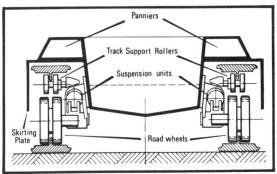

Above: Fig 2 Hull section and suspension.

Left: A new powerpack being fitted into the engine compartment of a Chieftain tank. The pack is suspended under the crane of a FV434 fitter's vehicle, belonging to 7th Field Workshop at the British Army Training Unit, Suffield, Canada. / *Crown copyright*

19

weight. The aggressive tread needed in war for good off-road performance conflicts with the smooth tread needed in peacetime to minimise road damage. Designs which give long life are usually heavy and involve high initial cost, so the true criterion to apply is whole life costs. The design originally selected was a dry pin, all-steel track similar to Centurion, but rubber pads had to be added in 1960 to meet the Federal German Government veto on the use of steel shod tracks on their roads. The cost and weight penalties of this change were unavoidable but to avoid loss of off-road performance the pads were made detachable on the assumption, perhaps unrealistic, that they would be removed before going to war.

The Hull Shell

The hull shell was designed to suit a driver who reclined in the closed down position so it was lower than Centurion at the front, which permitted the armour to be better sloped. Firing trials against the front of Centurion had shown that the driver's roof plate and its joint with the upper nose or glacis plate were vulnerable to the downward blast from a direct hit by an HE shell on the turret front. This form of attack was unlikely, but the weakness had to be avoided in Chieftain. By seating the driver centrally and making the hull front as an armour casting, the joint was avoided and the upper nose armour was blended through to the base of the turret ring without a horizontal roof, except in the area of the hatch, and here the casting was designed to withstand attack which would have disrupted a Centurion. The downward blast effects were also much reduced because the near vertical turret front of Centurion was replaced by a well sloped front on the Chieftain turret. By sloping the hull side plates as Centurion the joint with the belly plate was kept out of the cone of high blast pressure from track detonated mines. The hull belly was made shallow vee shape, to give maximum space where it was needed in the centre for the engine. The vee form reduced drag when moving with the belly plate on mud. Panniers over the tracks were made integral with the hull, thus adding strength and supporting the large turret ring which extended out over the tracks.

The Turret Shell

The choice of the turret as a fabrication made from a front casting and a rear part of rolled plate was influenced by a number of factors. The heavy frontal armour of Chieftain's turret was made possible, at an acceptable weight, by making its back much thinner than Centurion's, which was very thick — more for the weight needed for turret balance than for protection. Rolled plate was more suitable for the thinner

rear armour than casting. The features which enabled Chieftain's turret to be balanced although it had thick frontal and thin rear armour, were its large diameter ring, well sloped front armour, gun trunnions as far back as possible, no gun mantlet and a long bustle. Dispensing with the conventional gun mantlet saved weight and improved immunity. It overcame the hazard of a firepower kill which could result from a mantlet pinned by a partly penetrating shot or from gun trunnions damaged by loads transferred from a strike on the mantlet. The immunity of the mantle-less turret was proved by firing trials. The turret shell was designed so that the driver could always escape through his roof hatch.

Protection

The worldwide development of powerful anti-tank weapons made protection all round the tank impractical, so the frontal arc, where attack from anti-tank weapons was most likely, had to be the most heavily armoured and elsewhere immunity was required against lesser attacks such as shell splinters and machine gun fire. Weapon experts and intelligence staffs assessed weapon development and estimated the attacks which the new tank could face during its lifespan and thus established the level of protection needed for its frontal arc. Protection against kinetic energy (KE) attacks presented no particular problems with the well sloped hull and turret fronts. Penetration by the hollow charge weapons was much harder to prevent, especially by those of large diameter carried by anti-tank guided missiles.

Designs of spaced armour had been studied for many years and in 1954 concepts were drawn, incorporating the best then known. They were judged to involve too much development risk for the uncertain performance of the armour. For the lifespan of Chieftain the KE threat was expected to be greater than hollow charge, so armour was selected to give the best KE protection but steps were taken to lessen the effects of hollow charge. Skirting plates protected the hull sides and the reinforced casing of the bagged charge containers neutralised the effects of hollow charge spall. Ammunition fires have always been a major hazard to tanks, causing loss of crews and lowering morale. The water jacketed ammunition containers significantly reduced this hazard. The engine compartment fire hazard was reduced by using the new detection and suppression techniques developed for aircraft. The tank's armour gives a large measure of protection against the blast, heat, flash and radiation effects of a nuclear attack. The hazard of radioactive dust from contaminated ground was dealt with by filtering the air pumped in to pressurise the crew compartment. The filtration system could also deal with chemical and biological agents.

20

2. On Trial

During 1962 crews from the 1st and 5th Royal Tank Regiments, were posted from Germany to the Equipment Trials Wing (ETW) at Bovington (now called the Armoured Trials and Development Unit), for training on the prototype Chieftains. The aim was that two tanks would then be sent that winter to the two regiments which were stationed in Hohne and Fallingbostel, to continue the trials in BAOR (British Army of the Rhine). Gunnery, and D&M (Driving and Maintenance) instructors were sent by the two regiments to ETW, Sergeants Chapman and Cornish from 1RTR and Sergeants Hayward-Cripps and Harriman from 5RTR. It is an interesting aside to note that all four are now commissioned, three as Quartermasters, so they were clearly carefully chosen. Before joining ETW, they spent a few days at the Fighting Vehicle Research and Development Centre (FVRDE) at Chertsey (now called the Military Vehicles and Engineering Establishment), learning as much as possible about the prototypes while they were being built. Brian Hayward-Cripps was the 5RTR gunnery expert and he remembers the period they spent at ETW well. He writes:

'During 1962 the trial crews moved to the RAC Centre, the D&M segment moved to Bovington, the Gunnery to Lulworth. OC of the Gunnery Trials Wing of ETW was Major Jack Parker RTR. The RSM was a WO1 in the 4th Hussars of Polish descent. There was one Chieftain squatting in the hangar, I can't remember its number, but all trials Chieftains were prefixed "W" and I worked only on W1-W5 during the entire trial. Ted Chapman and I were greeted on our first working session with the order to write the handbook on the 120mm, RMG and GPMG etc! As we had only a superficial knowledge, picked up at FVRDE, it took a lot of midnight oil and damaged fingers before we finally produced an aide memoire for prospective Chieftain crews.

'It was an exciting time for us all, working on the future main battle tank, and we enjoyed the trials and experiments with the REME, to whom the tank was just as new as it was to us. The three months we spent at Lulworth were basically for us to familiarise ourselves with the gunnery side, to fire an immense number of rounds and to assist in the monotonous task of racking up the mileage. The sight of Chieftains, with flashing amber lights on the turret and escorted by landrovers, became a familiar sight around Bovington and the road to Lulworth. The automotive side was plagued with defects on the gearbox which continually delayed the trials programme. An example of the unusual happened when I was driving out of the hangar area at Lulworth, heading for the ranges. I started out in first gear, slipped into second, and as I pushed into third, the tank gave a tremendous jump and stalled. The same thing happened twice more so I called Staff Sergeant Renouf, our 5RTR fitter, who soon had the decks up. He then told me to repeat the performance, but to keep my foot down on the accelerator and this I did. After a great jump when pushed into third the tank shot backwards in high reverse! Another gearbox required.

'The gunnery trials went fairly well, various drills, misfires, bombing-up tests, etc were devised. There was no circuit tester for the 120mm and a boffin who visited us said that a circuit was to be introduced which would show a voltage drop on a fitted voltmeter if the circuit was complete. This seemed to me a complicated way of testing a circuit and just something else to go wrong. So, in a fit of enthusiasm, I cut down a vent tube, drilled out the base to take a micro-bulb, popped it into the striker and it worked!'

The two prototype Chieftains arrived out in Germany in late December 1962, one going to each regiment as planned. An intensive programme of trials had been mapped out and the 1RTR tank was to be committed mainly to the automotive tests. The timings of the trials were so critical that any major repairs were usually carried out at night, so that all would be ready for the next day's work. Tony Cornish recalls those days thus:

'At the start of trials there was a thick layer of snow and ice covering most of northern Germany. These conditions, whilst severely restricting the movements of the Centurions, had little affect on Chieftain. Cent

21

crews seemed strangely reluctant to accept offers of a tow from us! However, as there was no form of heating in Chieftain, it quickly became difficult for us to smile at stranded, but warm, Cent crews. As the weather got warmer and the area muddier, we found that Chieftain was tending to bog down in the well used Cent tracks on the Saltau Training Area, so Centurion road wheels and suspension springs were fitted — what happened to the "low silhouette"? On one long road run a gearbox high pressure hose split — I can recommend WD issue masking tape to any garage!'

Over in 5RTR Brian Hayward-Cripps had taken delivery of his new Chieftain:
'We paired the Chieftain with a Mark 7 Centurion and everything the Chieftain did, the Centurion had to do — if it could — with the exception of mileage, which just the Chieftain did. The security was fairly severe. The tank was housed in a nominated hangar, which was guarded 24 hours a day. No private photographs were allowed and the Chieftain was always escorted by at least one Ferret scout car, normally two. The great security cry was — "Watch out for Soxmis* and photographers". I was mainly concerned with gunnery, but took my turn with my crew, to put on the mileage. All kit, metadynes, sights, stabiliser and searchlight (covered) were running all the time during movement. There was very little running with the gun in the crutch.

'During the three months we trialled the tank, there was always snow and ice on the roads and cross-country. This gave the Cent 7 great problems and gave us the great delight of charging around on our

* Soxmis — The Soviet Military Mission.

rubberised tracks, passing the Cents sliding all over the roads and not getting up even slight inclines. But the Chieftain was not as good during the mobility trials, especially when jockeying from one fire position to another. One of the main reasons is that there was normally a dense film of oil (OM13) over the steering brake discs — caused by a constant series of leaks — so the steering levers had to be applied several time to "burn-off" the excess of oil before the tank could be turned. We found that the only answer was to start the day off by squirting a fire extinguisher over the brake discs to remove the oil.

'During the night driving phase we suffered like other motorists, from the arrogance of the drivers of the huge German lorries, who always drove on the crown of the road. We found that, as we approached them in the Chieftain, the answer was a quick flick on the switch to open the armoured shutter of the searchlight, one more and the infra-red cover was opened and a lot of candle-power was beamed into the lorry driver's eyes, causing chaos! The word obviously got around and we soon found that most drivers tended to pull in and let us pass. Gearboxes were the main headache, the main engines worked fairly well, but the gearboxes broke down often.

'The gunnery side went smoothly, no real problems except for the rammer and the charge containers. We all hated the rammer, it slowed down loading to an unacceptable degree for us "three in the air" Centurion types. It constantly failed mechanically and on one occasion, on the ranges it wouldn't stop ramming even when we had switched it off! The charge containers were always leaking, or the rain got into them, and it was a constant battle trying to keep them dry. And as we did all trials fully "bombed-up" it was a chore unloading each time to dry out the charge bins. It had

Left: PP1, an early model of the Chieftain. / *Tank Museum*

Right: Early production model Chieftain P4. / *Crown copyright*

Below: Early production model Chieftain P5 crosses a Centurion tank bridge. / *IWM*

Bottom: A Chieftain Mark 1 goes through its paces at a demonstration given at FVRDE in August 1963. Note the armoured box on the front to hide the slope of the glacis plate from prying eyes, also the split lid of the commander's cupola in the raised position. / *Soldier*

Above: Chieftain on Exercise Dryfoot (sand trials) in the Yuma desert, USA. / *Crown copyright*

become obvious to us during the Lulworth trials that the loader/operator was going to be very pushed to maintain a fast loading speed for very long. He had so much to do, what with the 120mm, the coax, RMG and vent tubes etc. We suggested to the boffins that a form of sparkplug should be used instead of the vent tube to ignite the charge. We were told that experiments had been carried out on this but that it had failed.

'After experiencing constant rammer defects, I suggested that we attempted to ram with the charge. It meant that, instead of the loader placing the projectile in the breech entrance and then operating the rammer to load fully, the loader would now push the projectile as far into the breech as he could, finally forcing it home with the charge. As you can imagine, hands were held up in horror and forecasts of what would happen ranged from buckling the charge to exploding it! One comment was that if the loader, in his haste, rammed the charge back to front, the igniter pad would explode. After carrying out my own trial, by loading an inert HESH using a charge and banging out the proj, then repeating the process, it was quite evident that the idea was a goer. To ensure that it was safe, I also arranged to drop a charge, igniter pad downwards, from the top of the high control tower on Range 21 at Hohne, on to the concrete hard standing below. The charge did not ignite and stood up to the shock of contact very well. It was then that we disconnected and removed the rammer and carried on loading by hand.

'A consequence of this was that, during a visit by General Liardet, who was to become Deputy Master General of Ordnance and was thus vitally interested in the trial, he noticed the rammer lying in the corner of the hangar. After a series of questions on our loading drill, he went slightly beserk, talking about all the £100,000s it had cost to produce the electro-mechanical rammer! However, we persuaded him that ours was a faster and less expensive method of ramming.'

1RTR also had their problems with the dreaded rammer and Tony Cornish told me that during the sustained firing trial their rammer broke down and had to be mended with masking tape (to seal down various switches) and a two-foot length of broom handle (to replace the rammer)! The boffins watching the trial had no knowledge of these 'improvisations' until after the trial had been successfully concluded and, when told, then expressed some doubt as to the validity of the trial, whereupon the loader, a fairly hefty (and very perspiring) lad called Corporal 'Spike' Rogers, invited them to see if they could do better! During another firing trial at 5RTR Sergeant Bob Harriman lost his eyebrows when the obturators blew. Being the D&M expert he was relatively inexperienced in gunnery, and when the flash from the obturators occurred, he didn't realise what was happening and couldn't understand the rapid evacuation of the gunner and loader! He was quite indignant when told what had happened as no one had ever told him it was dangerous to fire a Chieftain!

Brian Hayward-Cripps continues his reminiscences with this fascinating and graphic account of the closed-down trial:

'During the latter part of the trial, 1st and 5th RTR Chieftains were involved in a 5RTR exercise on the Soltau Training Area. I don't think that temperatures ever rose above freezing and the whole area was thick snow and ice. I remember one incident vividly. It was when both Chieftains were on the western side of the main wooded area in Area 2 and tank hunting parties were trying to find us. Using our IR sights we watched two groups thrusting their way through the waist-high

snow, then flicked the switch and illuminated them with the searchlight on white light, whereupon they dived for cover. We would then go back to IR and watch them groping their way out of the snowdrifts! It was a good exercise apart from the weather, and being on the Chieftains while everyone was on "old fashioned" Centurions, gave the crews a high morale. My own morale took a dive, however, when setting off back to barracks along the Wietzendorf corridor to Fallingbostel.

'We had passed the complete Regiment as they slid about on the icy roads, whilst our rubber padded tracks enabled us to drive safely without slipping. Then, to my utter disgust, my gearbox went and my crew and I had to sit looking forlorn as the Regiment charged by. The crews, of course, making very rude remarks — and signs!

'The culmination of the three month trial was a 72-hour "closed-down" exercise. 1RTR's tank was off the road so we had to do the trial alone. It basically comprised spending 72 hours closed down inside the tank, with an outside crew to carry out any external maintenance, refuelling, etc. All equipment had to remain on throughout the full period. At least 10 hours motoring was required during every 24-hour period over a variety of cross-country, roads and tracks. Tasks would be given on the radio, such as: "Take up a defensive position at Grid Reference...; move to cross roads at Grid...; take up an observation position at Grid... and report on enemy movements." The crew had to eat, sleep and carry out all bodily functions without leaving the tank. The turret and driver's hatches were not to be opened. At the end of the period, the tank was to move to the Hohne Gunnery Ranges and fire all its ammunition in a comprehensive series of shoots.

'My main memories of the trial were of the cold and the difficulties of four people living in such close proximity for so long. During daylight and for several periods at night, we motored all over the Fallingbostel/Hohne range area, always closed down, always responding to an order. It gave the crew a lot of pleasure to come charging along a road flat out, gun waving around on travelling stabiliser, no one to be seen on the tank. On one occasion we came thundering along a range road, down from Range 9, on to the public road at Ostenholtz, and, at a large clump of trees, came upon an "O" group in progress from a German Corps HQ. The "O" group, vehicles and men, scattered in all directions as we bore down on them. Our back-up crew told us later that the Germans thought that it was an unmanned tank out of control!

'The tank quickly became smelly and untidy, even with the strictest control, and we soon had numerous plastic bags containing human and food waste. It is not easy to take off parka, trousers etc to have a "crap" in the confines of a Chieftain turret, in the presence of the rest of the crew. The most unfortunate guy was the gunner who had to change places with the loader before he could relieve himself. We found that having the internal cooking pot and kettle was a bonus, but soon discovered that because of it all our compo could only be heated — it wasn't possible to fry the tinned sausages and appetites soon disappeared. It was a strange feeling to be in position at night carrying out wireless watch, two on and two off, and being able to see the back up crew bivvying up close by in relative comfort. The nights were extremely cold and, with no form of heating, our breath condensed and froze, coating the inside of the turret roof with ice. I found it impossible to sleep — a half-

25

frozen doze was the most I ever managed. We had, on previous trials, tried collapsible boards and hammocks, but they were not a success and there was nowhere to stow them inside the turret anyway. The driver, with his super reclining seat, could wriggle into a sleeping bag and drop off, but it was "snuggle into a parka, curl up somewhere and *try* to drop off" for the rest of us.

'The closed down trial started on a Friday morning. During the afternoon of the Saturday, the loader, while stripping the breech block as part of a secondary trial, cut the ball of his left thumb quite badly. I bandaged it and asked on the radio for a doctor, congratulating the loader on his coming escape from the trial. But it was not to be. The MO arrived, the loader's hatch was opened just sufficient for him to stick his arm out. His wound was stitched and an anti-tetanus injection given, then it was arm back inside, hatch closed and soldier on!

'It was on the Sunday afternoon, while we were driving across the ranges on yet another task, that the Commanding Officer, Lt-Col Winter Anstey, arrived in his Champ and asked me by radio if we wanted to continue. The reason he asked was that it had been an extremely cold night — 20° below — and it had taken a lot of revs to pull the tank off the ground as we were frozen in solid, but thanks to the rubber inserts we weren't irretrievably stuck. We were cold, dirty and tired, but it was less than 24 hours to the end, so we carried on. It re-emphasised what I had found in Korea in the winter, that the cold saps not only strength but will as well. Cold crews begin to think more about keeping warm than carrying out their jobs. It was a mistake not to instal a heater inside Chieftain, and ever since the MOD have "farted-about" with heated suits, quilted underwear etc, none of which has solved the basic problem.

'A tired but mildly jubilant crew brought the Chieftain to a halt on Range 7A at about 0815 hours on the Monday. Looking through the episcopes, we saw that there was quite a lot of "top brass" about, but more important to our morale was that all the other trials crews from both regiments were there. Still closed down we got ready to shoot. Someone put a red flag on to the turret, the first targets were "puffed" and the first "Ranging Sabot" engagement started. We fired everything — 120mm, GPMG, RMG and multi-barrelled smoke, traversed the turret, restowed and fired again. Eventually the loader shouted "Ammunition expended", we checked "guns clear" and asked permission to open up. We clambered out, my rear was numb having been sitting on the commander's seat for so long. Our fitter's staff sergeant, Jim Renouf, came up to me and offered me an army flask, which he said was coffee with just a splash of rum. The crew were swigging hot drinks, so I

drank it all — just under a quart. I was then pointed in the direction of the Commanding Officer, who introduced me to a general, who asked the usual sort of questions. I felt remarkably light-headed, and soon realised I was more than a little drunk — the flask had contained rum with a splash of coffee.'

During 1966, 1RTR was also responsible for the hot weather trials in Aden as tank driver Corporal Dunne recalls:

'Two Chieftains arrived in Aden on 28 July 1966. We were stationed in Falaise Camp, Little Aden, at the time and I remember the day they arrived quite well. When we went down to the docks to collect them we were immediately impressed by their power and speed. They were too big to take over the Causeway, so we had to drive them all the way around the coast, past various Arab villages. The inhabitants came out to throw rocks as usual, but when they saw how fast we were going, they went rushing back into their houses. They had never seen speed like that out of a tank before and were absolutely terrified. Our tank, a Mark 2 numbered 02 EB 48, was always very reliable, whereas the other one (02 EB 44) always seemed to be going wrong, with oil leaks and pack failures. We liked to think that it was because we maintained our tank very carefully every day. One problem we did have in the early days was the engine clogging up with sand. The fine desert sand used to get through the oil filters. We cured the problem by replacing the OMD110 oil with OEP220, the other crew continued to use the original oil and I think this is why they had so many more problems than we did.

'One good feature of Chieftain we all noticed was its ability to go across soft sand and salt flats. With her extra speed and wider tracks the tank could negotiate places where Centurions would sink straight in. The trick was to get up a good speed, aim a course before you reached the salt flats and then go like hell without touching your sticks or brakes. On one occasion the other driver did touch his sticks and the track cut into the surface of the salt. The tank went straight in and it took us about five hours to get it out.

'One day we went into the desert to do some firing. The object was to fire as many rounds as possible in one minute. Just as we started shooting the air conditioner in the turret packed up. I was in the driving seat, so I didn't know anything was wrong, because I still had fresh air coming in, but as the last round went down range the commander, Sergeant Stevens, croaked "Head for Ginger Gray" who was our medic. I realised that something was wrong, so sped over to the medical vehicle. The turret was so full of smoke and fumes that the whole turret crew had collapsed. We got them out and after a while they all recovered OK.'

3. Into Service

'It has always been the great strength of the 11th Hussars that we have honoured the past, but worked for and looked forward to the future. We did this when we changed from horses to armoured cars in 1928 and again in 1961/62 when we converted from armoured cars to tanks. During both changes we grumbled, but got on with the job. We became the example to all other cavalry regiments in our armoured car work in our first change, and, in our change to tanks, second to none amongst armoured regiments serving in Germany. Again we have a challenge. This time it is not a change of role, but a new and untried tank, the "Chieftain", which we have to master; and lead the way for others to follow. Six of these very expensive and highly complicated machines arrived in November 1966, and the remainder will arrive in batches during the first few months of 1967. The whole regiment has got to learn enough about them in order to exercise with them in June, and to fire them on the ranges in July. This is no easy task, but we are all confident that we will acquit ourselves well.'

So wrote Colonel Peter Hamer, then Commanding Officer of the 11th Hussars, in the editorial to the 1966 edition of the *XI Hussar Journal*. Events were to show that once again the Cherry Pickers would live up to their reputation of getting on with the job and making a success of it. I have been very fortunate in persuading various members of the Eleventh, including Peter Hamer, to let me have their reminiscences of those stirring days when the new tanks arrived. He writes:

'It had been planned to introduce Chieftain into my Regiment before I assumed command, but as events turned out this was not to be, and the first tanks arrived after I had been in command for about a year. Steps had been taken in preparation by forming a special unit at the RAC Centre, Bovington Camp, which had been tasked with ironing out some of the early teething trials. This was a joint 11th Hussar and 17th/21st Lancer* venture, and a number of the most

* 17/21L were scheduled to be the second regiment to be equipped with Chieftain.

qualified officers, NCOs and men from both regiments were seconded to staff this unit.

'I was personally thrilled by the challenge, and the honour shown to the regiment in being chosen, and we were all determined that Chieftain would be a success. An early warning system was developed so that all information should be fed back, commented on and sent to the appropriate authorities. This started long before the first tank appeared in Hohne. Information was regularly passed to us from the RAC Centre, from the FVRDE and elsewhere, and it was prove invaluable when "D-Day" arrived. There were many practical measures which had to be taken before the tanks appeared in Germany, not only in Hohne and Sennelager, but also in ordnance and ammunition depots etc. Spares, ammunition and many other items would have to be stockpiled in advance and, because both regiments would be operating two types of tank for some time, storage capacity had to be increased. The sighting equipment was, at this stage, highly classified and being aware of the efficiency of the Eastern bloc intelligence systems, special stores had to be built, as all sights were removed each night. Extra work had to be done on the tank parks to make them secure and to prevent unauthorised entry. This was proved very necessary as more than one attempt was made to break in. Indeed, one "observer" was put to flight by the Brigade Commander's wife one day while out riding! They shadowed us for the best part of a year on every exercise.

'The whole conversion programme had to be planned in great detail, without necessarily knowing all the facts — we had a forecast of delivery dates, but naturally, as these were issued a long time ahead, one had to remain very flexible, because no one could say precisely at what date any troop or squadron would be complete. All this had to be done with a background of applications for extra range space and training areas, and I can't speak too highly of the various staffs who worked wonders to meet our ever changing requests. Indeed, the work of the Staffs and Technical Services throughout the conversion period was beyond reproach — everyone seemed determined to smooth our task. There was a certain amount of internal

reorganisation required as it was essential that the first squadron should have the benefit of the best tradesmen, although very little cross-posting was necessary. Nevertheless, many people had to be sent on courses to Bovington and Lulworth, and this left the regiment very thin on the ground for a long time before any machinery appeared. Again, we were extremely grateful for the extra work done by RAC Centre and many others for providing all the courses and other help we needed. An example of the sort of problem with which we were faced, was that Chieftain was to run on diesel (at least we were thankful that the multi-fuel idea had been dropped before we were in the market). However, this meant extra fuel pumps in the tank park and particular care in the canned fuel dumps as a mixture could be fatal! This of course applied even more when we had to take to the field.

'Eventually clearance was received for the tank to be introduced into service and, while it had been motoring around Bovington Heath and FVRDE for a considerable time, it is a very different situation when a new piece of equipment is issued to troops. By this time, several of our newly trained men had returned and many strange tales were told, some of which filled me with gloom. However, the great day arrived and a large reception party went down to the sidings to see the first batch. The first thing which struck me about Chieftain was that it looked good — usually any service equipment which looks good is good. It was low and streamlined compared with Centurion which

now looked like something out of the Ark to my eyes. The tanks were started up and driven off the railway flats. My next impression was, apart from the initial burst of blue smoke, how quiet it was. The crews got in and drove to the tank park, and I was surprised to find how difficult it was to keep up in my staff car! Naturally, the drivers wanted to show off and they had the whole regiment to show off to, plus quite a lot of Hohne Garrison and heaven knows how many spies! The way Trooper Wilkinson threw the first tank round the park was most impressive and frightening! One aspect of reorganisation which caused a certain amount of concern to the CO, was that he had, quite rightly, to stick rigidly to our establishment and this meant, among other things, that the CO had to go to war in a tank — not universally popular among other regiments as well as my own! However, I soon became converted and really enjoyed it, although I did have rather too many mounts: tank, staff car, landrover, FV432, helicopter and scout car. All had different roles and it did make the incumbent rather fitter than usual, having to jump from one to another!

'Gradually the tanks started to arrive in threes and fours. One thing which helped us in these early stages was that we were not inundated with visitors, though this did not last all that long, and our visitors book soon needed replacement. By the time that C Squadron was complete we had a pretty good idea of Chieftain's performance and many trials began, chiefly in the areas of movement and gunnery. As far as the first was concerned, I was determined to prove that the tank was not underpowered. We set up a measured half mile outside the main NAAFI and

tested all the tanks over this, once they had started to bed in. The results were very encouraging and one was timed at 35mph, which naturally was pinched by the Commanding Officer. I well remember scaring the daylights out of a rather fat German in a Mercedes 3000, by leaving him for dead at the traffic lights near Soltau! It soon became clear to me that not only was the maximum speed more than expected, but that the average over a distance was considerably improved. I remember having a violent argument about this with our Brigade Commander, Dick Worsley, who would not believe me.

'On our first exercise with 7th Armoured Brigade, I eventually persuaded him to put my tanks at the front of the brigade column in a 40-mile night march, the reverse of the normal procedure, and proved my point by passing the release point half an hour before anyone else turned up, recce troops and all. Chieftain was not only quicker across country, but a considerably more comfortable ride than Centurion and, even more important, over really bad ground it could leave a Leopard for dead, despite all the latter's engine and weight advantage. Their crews just could not survive the speed as they were chucked about so much.

'Gunnery was even more fascinating and, despite all the dreadful stories we were told about the speed of loading and other horrors, we eventually got the speed down below Centurion and managed to acquire an "Outstanding" report on our first annual firing. We would obviously have preferred to start with the laser sight, but had to persevere with the ranging gun — this had one useful side effect in that, during many hours of tests on the ranges with individual tanks

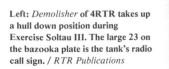

Left: *Demolisher* of 4RTR takes up a hull down position during Exercise Soltau III. The large 23 on the bazooka plate is the tank's radio call sign. / *RTR Publications*

Right: Tanks of 4RTR supporting infantry APCs, roar into the attack. / *RTR Publications*

Below: An excellent shot of a Royal Hussar Chieftain travelling at speed through muddy terrain on the Sennelager Training Area, April 1976. / *Crown copyright*

under Johnny Lewis, our Gunnery Officer, we devised a scheme for first round hits at extreme ranges, using a combination of the ranging gun and the HESH scale when firing APDS.

'I was so lucky to command when I did as many of the notorious engine difficulties did not appear until after my time, but I think I can say that the majority of problems were given undeserved publicity. Enormous credit for the success of Chieftain was due to every soldier, NCO and officer who did so much to help. I used to hold periodic meetings of representatives of all ranks who were encouraged to criticise and give advice, and all this information was fed into the machinery as well as the normal methods of reporting . . .'

Johnny Lewis, the Regimental Gunnery Officer, had this to say about the main armament:
'It was a fabulous gun and probably capable of far more than we expected of it. Certainly the accuracy of APDS was staggering and on a number of occasions we practiced with my regimental instructors well over the ranges designed for Dot 5. Using imaginary dots we achieved total accuracy up to 3,000m and more. Much against the rule book we fired a demonstration to the Danish Armoured Corps in Denmark up to ranges in excess of 3,000m with complete success and even I was surprised how good our gunners were! On the debit side, the gun needed far greater care and cleaning and I wondered just how long our crews would have kept things working under battle conditions. It was a complex weapon and the firing system, with exacting cartridge alignment, posed problems.'

31

Above: Driver training at Bovington. A Chieftain at the RAC Centre. / *Crown copyright*

Above right: Cold and dirty after a busy night, this Royal Hussar crew move off for yet another day's exercising. / *Soldier*

Right: A good side view of a Chieftain taken during an exercise emphasises the length of the barrel of the main gun. / *Crown copyright*

My third Cherry Picker to recall those days is WO2 Brian Gormley, who is currently serving at the RAC Junior Leaders Regiment. He writes:

'I was lucky enough to be a member of the final acceptance trials team sent by the regiment to Bovington. The team consisted of two crews under Capt Villiers with myself and Sgt 'Arnold' Palmer as the two tank commanders. A similar team from the 17th/21st Lancers also took part. The end of the trials virtually coincided with the issue of the first tanks to the regiment, so those of us on the trials team had nearly a year's intensive training and experience of the vehicle before it came into general service. I like to think that this experience, which we passed on to our comrades, helped save many man-hours in repairs and the prevention of breakdowns, through having an inkling of what was liable to go wrong and how to stop it happening. We had learned, after many cold nights on the Bovington driving area, just what 'bits' were liable to drop off or fracture at an awkward moment. Most of these seem to have occurred at 4.30pm on a Friday afternoon, just as one was looking forward to the weekend!

'When we returned to the regiment from Bovington, we knew already that we were to be the first unit with the new tank and naturally there was great excitement and speculation about it. Rumours abounded about its complexity and reliability/unreliability as compared with Centurion. Most of these stories came, as usual, from a "bloke who had spoken to another bloke at Bovvy". However, everyone — RHQ to the pig farm — was eagerly awaiting their first glimpse of Chieftain. Appetites were whetted by countless photos and diagrams plastered on noticeboards throughout the barracks. In the tank park, Centurions, which had for years been nurtured by their crews and had now been prepared for handover to Ordnance, or to less fortunate regiments, lay ignored at the back of the hangars.

'C Squadron, under Major Michael Allenby, was to be the first squadron to be re-equipped. The great day arrived when news came that the train carrying the first four tanks had reached the Bergen railway

Above left: Chieftains of 3RTR move out of Bhurtpore Barracks, Tidworth, at the start of Exercise Mayflower, May 1978. / *Soldier*

Left: 2 BRAVO negotiates a tricky roundabout during Exercise Mayflower, a battle group exercise held on and around Salisbury Plain, May 1978. / *Soldier*

Above: The long and the short of it! A Chieftain dwarfs this CVR(T) Scorpion, the British Army's latest armoured reconnaissance vehicle. / *FPT Industries*

sidings. The trials crews, who were the only people yet able to move the tanks, were driven down to the sidings personally by Major Allenby. After some careful manoeuvring off the flats they drove to Haig Barracks with some comment (still applicable today!) on the amount of exhaust fumes being thrown out. Virtually the whole of the regiment was waiting for us in the tank park, plus many Dutchmen who shared the compound with us. I think there were a few of our neighbours from 2RTR as well, trying to look very blasé, as if they weren't a little indignant that the cavalry were getting the new toy before them!

'As soon as the new arrivals were backed into the hangars and switched off, they were covered from glacis to engine decks in bodies anxious to see at first hand what until then had only been a photo or an object of discussion. Curiosity gradually waned over the next week or so, as the remaining Chieftains arrived to bring us up to scale. By this time our instructors had returned from the conversion courses in UK and the retraining programme began in earnest. Gunnery training was, I think, rather less of a problem than D&M. After all, the shooting techniques were basically the same as for the 105mm Cent with ranging gun. It only required detailed instruction in the mechanics of the turret, main armament and machine guns to convert. D&M was more complex. There was the difference in diesel and petrol engines, in air cleaners, brakes and their servicing, plus the completely different techniques used in gear changing, to contend with. All the same these were quickly absorbed and the first field training took place soon after all crewmen had converted in their primary trades. On the whole, crews were delighted with the new tank. There were, of course, many breakdowns, but compared to Centurion they were not nearly so time consuming except that spares took a long time to appear.

'Cent still had its diehard supporters. Chieftain lacked crew space (apart from the driver) and its decks were certainly not as comfortable to kip on! These reactionaries tended to forget those bad features of the Cent, like main brake failure, plug changes, gear linkage jams and the physical effort in merely driving the machine. One aspect of Chieftain over which all crews enthused were the boiling vessels. Their speed to the boil and reliability compared with the antique issued previously meant that any well-organised crew had a constant source of hot water and "scoff". Two main sources of irritation, however, were: fan belt failures, which really were disgraceful in the frequency they occurred, and "gunge". Chieftain was, and still is, a dirty tank to work on. The engine compartment streamed with oil from various leaks and the mist emitted by the exhausts clung everywhere. It only took seconds for a crewman to change from being clean to looking like a tarbaby. I think that more than any other point this was the greatest criticism of the AFV.

'On the whole, though, during the first shakedown exercise on Soltau, the crews learned to live on the vehicle and appreciate the many minor improvements which made life easier, like fitted map reading lights and superior vision aids. The searchlight was a great plaything and irate squadron commanders would see their positions being given away by unthinking commanders twiddling the control knobs and inadvertently switching to white light! The searchlight was also a trap for unwary drivers, who forgot about the overhang and persistently parked too near to very tough trees. This resulted in some large repair bills before the point sunk home.

'With regard to servicing, some drivers, through their own enthusiasm and observation, became proficient enough to prepare the powerpack for lifting by themselves. This was a great boon to the fitters. You can imagine the relief felt by a "Bluebell" team when they arrived at a casualty to find half the job already done for them. The LAD (Light Aid Detachment REME) attached to the 11th at this time was probably the best I have ever worked with. They were completely integrated into the regiment and Capt Derbyshire and ASM Tocknell headed a team which had to convert even more rapidly than our crewmen. They were never stuck in any situation even though they had to improvise many times through lack of written instructions. EMERs were still in the process of being written for much of Chieftain's equipment.

'As the months went by endless discussions went on in the messes and squadron bars on all aspects of the tank. I think it is fair to say that the Eleventh felt at that time they were top of the tree, even if the rest of the Royal Armoured Corps didn't share that opinion! It is a great experience being unique, the only ones to possess a brand-new piece of equipment. Of course it didn't last and, by the autumn of 1967, the 17th/21st were starting to convert and other regiments would being the change-over in early 1968. In the meantime, Chieftain was still the object of much curiosity. Visitors continually came to the barracks or visited us on exercises and were given demonstrations of Chieftain's prowess. I remember one group of RAF fighter pilots who, after a short period of instruction, had the demo tank roaring all over the training area — they were much better than the normal trainee driver!

'We had great arguments with the Germans over the relative merits of Chieftain and Leopard, which had also just entered service. They liked to show off their tank's impressive cross-country performance, whilst we told them that the 105mm gun we had sold them was an antique. Nevertheless, we did have a sneaking regard for the Leopard engine and many of us felt that perhaps that was the kind of engine we needed to really make Chieftain as good as it could be.

'Open range firing was perhaps the greatest challenge we had to overcome. After all, the whole concept of the new tank was based around that huge gun. Problems still plagued us. The vent tube loader timing was critical for the whole loading sequence. Unfortunately, many misfeeds did arise, despite careful preparation by crews and gunfitters. Lack of experience had a lot to do with it, but in view of the many modifications which have since taken place, the equipment must have been faulty at times. Many crews bypassed this irritation by feeding the vent tubes by hand. This, in fact, did not cause a great deal of delay and one was confident that the gun would fire every time. Alas, later ammunition regulations forbade the removal of the tubes from their containers and the practice had to cease. But it was not all gloom by any means on the ranges and the crews were delighted with the gun when everything was going smoothly, although obscuration was a greater bugbear than with the 105mm. Range arcs were also much more restricted with the need for a greater template area. All in all, once experience had been acquired, the standard of equipment preparation improved enormously and mechanical faults lessened. In the end malfunctions became the exception and demonstrations of the effects of service ammunition against a hitherto undamaged Conqueror gave every one great confidence in the weapon.

'As I have said, we greatly enjoyed our short period of uniqueness while it lasted; that feeling of superiority when we passed another unit still equipped with Cents, the crews' envious glances as we motored by. It had to come to an end of course, and just about two years after the first Chieftains had arrived in Hohne we moved back to UK to amalgamate with the 10th Hussars at Tidworth to become the Royal Hussars. The AFV issued to the new regiment was, would you believe it, Centurion, and you can imagine the many long faces that there were on the tank park at Bhurtpore Barracks! It would be nearly four more years before we moved to Sennelager and that Chieftain became once more our tank.'

4. Basic Description

The Chieftain tank is a fully-tracked Armoured Fighting Vehicle of conventional design, with a forward compartment for the driver, a central fighting compartment for the commander, gunner and loader, and a rear compartment for the engine, gearbox and transmission. The driver is seated in the centre of the hull with a single piece 'lift and swing' hatch cover. His seat lets down to a reclining position when driving closed down. The rest of the crew are in a fully rotating turret, commander and gunner on the right and loader on the left. There are two openings in the turret roof, a pair of hatch covers on the left and the commander's cupola on the right with a single lid (the Mark 1 had a split lid). Main access to the rear compartment is via a series of top decking plates.

Salient features

A 120mm high velocity gun of extreme accuracy and outstanding ballistic performance using ammunition with separated charges. High speed of target engagement and a high probability of a first round kill, even at long ranges and against moving targets. A high degree of immunity against any enemy tank, present or future. A high degree of immunity to ammunition fires, if penetration should occur, by the use of special bins for stowing charges. Excellent cross-country

performance resulting in unequalled battlefield mobility and the retention by the crew of a high level of combat efficiency.

Firepower

The 120mm L11 (A2, A3 or A5) high velocity bagged charge gun, fitted with a fume extractor and thermal sleeve, is mounted centrally in the turret without a mantlet and stabilised in both azimuth and elevation. Bagged charge ammunition is used as it is both quicker and less tiring to handle and easier to stow. Using this ammunition the maximum rate of fire is 8-10 rounds in the first minute and six rounds/minute thereafter. The gun has a vertically sliding breech block which opens automatically on gun runout. Obturation is based on the use of ring seals, which prevent the escape of gas between the breech block and the chamber. The bagged charge has a powder igniter at the rear which is ignited by means of an electrically fired vent tube, 14 of which are held in a magazine in the vent tube loader on the breech ring. The ammunition is hand rammed into the breech. The main types of ammunition fired are: Armour Piercing Discarding Sabot (APDS), High Explosive Squash Head (HESH), Smoke, Illuminating and Canister. New types of ammunition are currently under

Fig 3 Chieftain general layout.

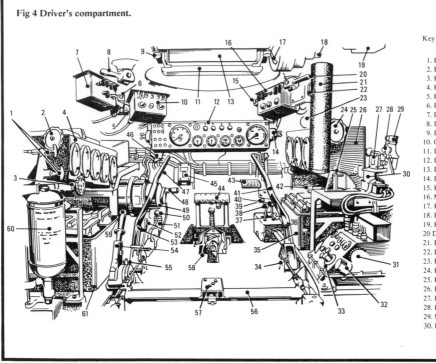

Fig 4 Driver's compartment.

development including new training rounds. Adequate ammunition is carried for a normal day's engagements, the charges being contained in their specially developed fireproof containers. 53 rounds (Mk 3 tank) and 64 rounds (Mk 5 tank) are carried.

In addition to the main armament, Chieftain carries the following other weapons: a Ranging Machine Gun, .50in calibre Browning L21A1, firing flashing-tipped trace ammunition; two 7.62mm General Purpose Machine Guns, one (L8A1) mounted coaxially with the main gun, the other (L37A1) on the cupola for the commander; two banks of six smoke discharger cups, one bank on each side of the turret; four Sterling machine carbines L2A3 (crew personal weapons); a signal pistol and various grenades (both coloured smoke and anti-personnel).

The tank is fitted with the Marconi Fighting Vehicle Gun Control System No 7 Mk 4, which has four modes of control — stabilised power, power, emergency battery and hand. IFCS — the Integrated Fire Control System — also made by Marconi Space and Defence Systems Ltd, is now being introduced (see Chapter 5). The sighting and fire control equipment is designed to enable the crew to engage targets quickly and accurately. Although the invidual items vary internally between the different marks of Chieftains, they always comprise:

Top right: View inside the driving compartment. / *Simon Dunstan*

Right and below: View of gunner's station.
/ *Wharton Engineers (Elstree) Ltd*

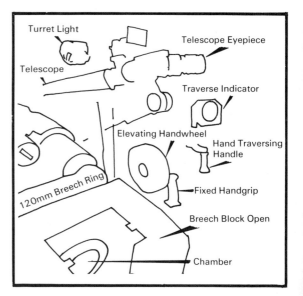

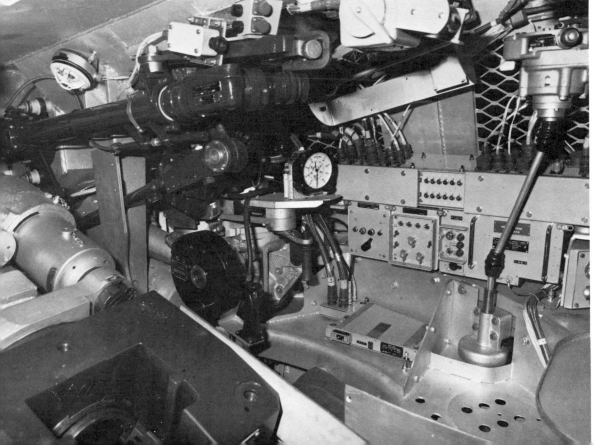

A periscopic sight for the commander mounted in his cupola, used for directing the gunner on to a target and incorporating a Projector Reticule Image which is located on the turret roof immediately in front of the cupola ring. The sight can also be used for observation and correction of fire by the commander.

Two sights for the gunner, one periscopic sight which protrudes through the turret roof and is his normal means of sighting, the latest version being the Barr and Stroud Tank Laser Sight (see Chapter 5); the standby is a telescopic sight which is fitted behind a small aperture in the turret frontal armour. The gunner has a quadrant fire controller, complete with clinometer and range scales (for semi-indirect and indirect shooting) and an electrically driven traverse indicator for applying line corrections.

Observation equipment for the commander consists of nine periscopes mounted in his all-round traversing cupola. The loader has a single periscope which can be rotated through 360°, while the driver has a periscope giving him vision over a frontal arc which he uses when driving closed down. At night, both the commander and gunner can replace their day periscopic sights with infra-red equipment. Other IR equipment mounted on the turret is:

The 2kW IR/white light searchlight mounted on the left-hand side.

The commander's IR/WL spotlight on his cupola.

An IR detector gives both an audible and visual warning when the tank is being illuminated by enemy IR.

The driver has an IR periscope for use at night in conjunction with IR headlights. In view of the ease of detection and the limited performance of the IR, passive night viewing aids, such as Image Intensification, are being introduced. When this has been done the IR equipment, including the searchlight will be dispensed with.

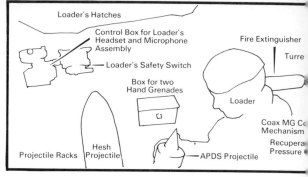

Protection

The nose section is cast, with the hull sides, rear and floor being welded into place. The turret is also cast. The internal volume of the AFV has been reduced and the weight thus saved used to thicken the armour over the frontal arc. Chieftain has a higher proportion of its weight devoted to armour than any other comparable tank in service. The thickness and slope of the frontal armour gives the tank the ability to withstand both heavy anti-tank and artillery fire. The sloping hull sides add to the level of immunity from mines, while the skirting/bazooka plates give a level of protection against small calibre hollow charge weapons. Of course the introduction of Chobham armour for the Mark 2 Shir derivative of Chieftain will dramatically improve its level of protection (see Chapter 6).

The tank is fitted with an NBC ventilation system pack No 6 Mk 1 or Mk 2 (earlier models of the tank were fitted with Pack No 2). This pack gives the crew protection against nuclear fall out, bacteriological or chemical attacks, thus obviating the need to wear either respirators or personal protective clothing inside the AFV. When closed down the crew have complete protection against nuclear heat flash, while the thick

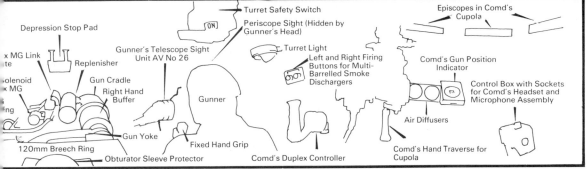

Depression Stop Pad

Turret Safety Switch

Periscope Sight (Hidden by Gunner's Head)

Episcopes in Comd's Cupola

x MG Link te

Replenisher

Gunner's Telescope Sight Unit AV No 26

Turret Light

Left and Right Firing Buttons for Multi-Barrelled Smoke Dischargers

Comd's Gun Position Indicator

olenoid x MG

ng

Gun Cradle

Right Hand Buffer

Gunner

Control Box with Sockets for Comd's Headset and Microphone Assembly

120mm Breech Ring

Gun Yoke

Fixed Hand Grip

Air Diffusers

Obturator Sleeve Protector

Comd's Duplex Controller

Comd's Hand Traverse for Cupola

Above: Panoramic view inside the turret, looking towards the front, with l to r: the loader picking up an APDS projectile; 120mm breech ring (NB neither the coax GPMG nor the RMG are fitted in this photo); gunner looking through his periscopic sight; foreshortened view of the commander's station, so that his duplex controller looks to be much nearer the gunner than it actually is in real life.
/ Crown copyright

Left: Driver's hatch, with 'lift and swing' lid in closed position. Note also the driver's periscope with windscreen wipers.
/ Crown copyright

41

Left: Commander's cupola No 15 from the rear with the lid closed. The commander's GPMG is fitted in its mounting, but not loaded (box for ammo belt on LHS of gun). Note also: the periscopic sight sticking up above the ring, with the spotlight mounting on its right; cupola episcopes each with its own wipers and wiper motors. / *Crown copyright*

Below: Commander's cupola with lid open, gunner's periscope and PRI from the front. Note: no commander's periscopic sight — wiper unit is cleaning fresh air! — gunner's periscopic sight with armoured shield raised, head of Projector Reticule Image (PRI) can be seen in front of the cupola and to the side of the gunner's periscope. / *Crown copyright*

Right: Lifting the rear decks. This photograph gives a good impression of the size and weight of the rear decking on a Chieftain. The gun crutch is visible, hanging down below the driver's left boot. / *Crown copyright*

Below right: Fig 5 Layout of main engine, automotive and electrical components.

armour plate and rigidity of the structure, give a high degree of protection against nuclear radiation and blast. The tank is fitted with a Graviner Firewire automatic fire detection and extinguishing system for the engine, whilst the bagged charges are kept in separate pressurised water jacketed containers to reduce fire risk.

Mobility

The Chieftain powerpack is the Leyland L60 six-cylinder (12 vertically opposed pistons) two-stroke compression engine, which has been continually improved and uprated from 585bhp (Mk 4A) to 650bhp (Mk 5A), to 720bhp (Mk 7A) and finally to 750bhp (Mk 8A). The L60 is a multi-fuel engine, but is normally run on diesel. The Shir derivatives will be fitted with the Rolls-Royce CV12 engine, which produces 1,200bhp at 2,300rpm (see Chapter 7). A Merritt Wilson Type TN12 Mk 5 combined gearbox and steering unit, combines the Wilson epicyclic gear change principle with the Merritt steering system, transmitting the drive to single reduction final drive units. The unit has six forward and three effective reverse ratios, of which only two are used, the third being used as an emergency gear along with one selected gear from the forward range. For the Shir, the new David Brown TN37 automatic transmission and the Dunlop hydro-pneumatic suspension are being developed. Steering is by means of hydraulically operated disc brakes. Main brakes are of the power assisted hydraulically operated disc type and a

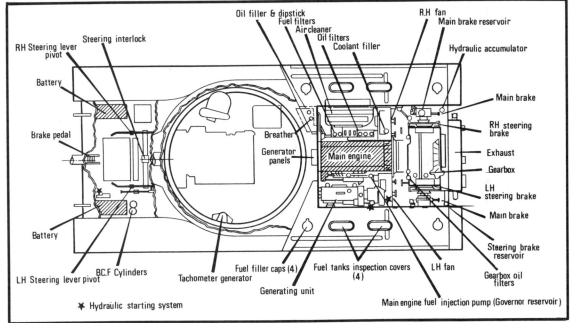

43

manually operated handbrake is provided for parking. A three-cylinder two-stroke compression ignition auxiliary H30 engine is also fitted, providing hydraulic power drive to the fan on the power pack via a free wheel device and a low temperature cold starting facility for the main engine. It also drives a 350A 24V ac alternator, running in parallel with the 150A alternator on the main engine as required. Four 12V batteries, connected in series/parallel provide 24V for the main electrical services and two additional 12V batteries supply 24V for the radio services.

Communications

The basic radio equipment comprises the Larkspur range of radios, one C42 and one B47, with an A-type harness being the normal fit. This also gives intercommunication between all members of the crew and to the infantry/tank telephone mounted on the rear of the AFV. A remote control unit with 200yd (180m) of cable is also provided. The AFV can accept field conversion kits for both Command and Control roles (ie basically an additional C42 set for SHQ and RHQ tanks). The Clansman range of radio equipment is currently being introduced (see Chapter 8).

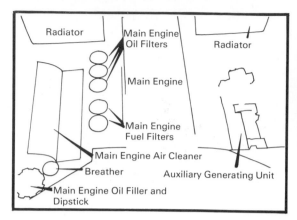

Above and right: Close-up of the L60 engine, with the radiators in the raised position. / *Crown copyright*

Below: Close-up of the NBC pack on the rear of the turret. The door, when unbolted, swings open on the hinges (on LHS). Note air intake lourvres on RHS. / *Crown copyright*

Below right: Close-up of the gearbox, showing the left and right hand steering brakes on either side. / *Crown copyright*

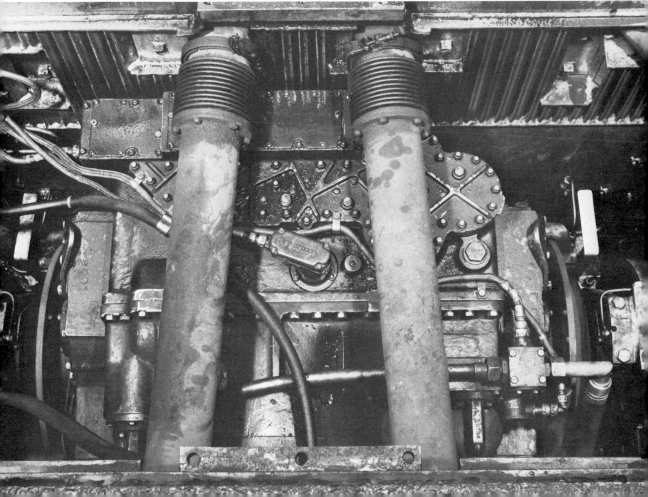

DIFFERENT MARKS

Mark 1: Original basic preproduction vehicle. It has been used for training. It was fitted with the Mk 4A (585bhp) engine, uprated to 650bhp during reconditioning. Majority have been converted to Mk 1/1 and Mk 1/2. Only 40 built. First issued in 1963.

Mark 1/2: Basic Mark 1 AFV converted by the REME, with improved cupola and roof mounted machine gun for commander, improved exhaust and rear hull sealing for deep wading; improved smoke dischargers; IR headlamps added.

Mark 2: L60 Mk 5A (650bhp) engine fitted and improved turret ballistic immunity. First model to enter operational service in November 1966 with the 11th Hussars.

Mark 3: Similar to the Mk 2, but has an H30 Mk 10A auxiliary generator giving improved hydraulic starting; Mk 6A engine gives improved reliability with the same bhp (650); provision for laser rangefinder; improved parking brake. Entered service 1969.

Mark 3/2: As for Mk 3, but with prototype turret/hull air cleaner breathing and provision for prototype laser equipment.

Mark 3S: Similar to Mk 3, but with production type turret/hull air cleaner breather and minor electrical improvements.

Mark 3/3: As for Mk 3, but with top rollers and idlers lubricated; strengthened suspension; production type turret/hull air cleaner breathing; improved NBC filtration pack (No 6 Mk 2); production laser mounting.

Mark 3/3(P): Export model of the Mk 3/3 for the Iranian Army from 1971.

Mark 5: As for Mk 3/3, plus uprated engine Mk 7A giving 720bhp (gross); new low loss exhaust system; generator air filters; Stage 5 charge bins; redistribution of stowage.

Mark 5/5(P): Export model of the Mark 5 for the Iranian Army.

Mark 5/5(K): Export model of the Mark 5 for Kuwait.

Mark 6: Mk 2 with new powerpack and modified RMG.

Mark 7: All Mk 3 models with improved engine and modified RMG.

Mark 8: Mk 3/3 with improved engine and modified RMG.

Note: All production gun tanks Mks 2, 3, 3/2, 3/S and 3/3 are to be improved to an automotive and fire control equipment standard equal to the Mk 5 ex-

production AFV. The Mks 1, 1/1 and 1/2 will have only automotive improvements.

All marks of Chieftain are to have automotive and fire control improvements. These include the fitting of the Tank Laser Sight, Muzzle Reference System, IFCS, cupola traverse and periscopic improvements, plus the commander's combined Day/Night fitment and associated modifications. The nomenclature of the various marks will alter as these mods are introduced, but once they have all been completed they will be known as follows:

Mark 2: becomes Mark 9
Mark 3, 3/G and 3/S: become Mark 10
Mark 3/3: becomes Mark 11
Mark 5: becomes Mark 12

Any tank with the letter (C) after its mark number has the Clansman basic harness installed.

Production and Lifespan

Following the experimental model P1 in 1959, six prototypes were delivered between July 1961 and April 1962. In May 1963, 40 Mark 1 preproduction models were produced. Also that month the British Ministry of Defence ordered 770 Chieftains from the Royal Ordnance Factory at Barnbow near Leeds and Vickers Armstrong Elswick works, the order to be completed by 1971. In 1971 Iran signed a contract for

Above: A good shot of the 120mm gun barrel with thermal sleeve. / *IWM*

Right: The Chieftain hull assembly line at the ROF Leeds. / *Crown copyright*

780 Chieftains, 707 of which were to be Mark 5/5(P). 73 Armoured Recovery Vehicles were also ordered. Iran ordered a further 150 MBTs in 1975 and Kuwait ordered a similar number that same year. In 1974 Iran signed a new contract for over 1,200 Shir Mark 2 tanks (with Chobham armour) and whilst waiting for delivery will receive 150 Shir Mark 1s. 175 modified ARVs were also ordered. The planned lifespan of Chieftain in the British Army will be until the mid-1980s, giving the tank a service lifespan of about 25 years which compares favourably with any previous main battle tank.*

* The recent troubles in Iran have led to the cancellation of the Shir contracts and to date it is not clear what will happen next.

Fume Extractor

Comd's MG

Comd's Spotlight

Searchlight

RMG

Telescope

Headlamps with IR Filters

03 EB 35

Left: Chieftain front view showing salient details. Note also rubber pads on tracks and sloped under armour. / *Crown copyright*

Right and below right: Back view of Chieftain showing main details. / *Crown copyright*

SPECIFICATION (Mark 5)

Weight laden: 54 tons combat-loaded
Shipping weight: 52 tons

Fire power

Main armament: 120mm OBL tank gun L11A7 fitted with thermal sleeve and fume extractor, firing APDS, HESH, smoke and training ammunition, etc
Secondary armament: two 7.62mm general-purpose machine gun, one co-axial with the main armament, and one on commander's cupola fired from under armour
Ammunition stowage: 64 rounds including 10 APDS projectiles stowed externally. All charges in special fire-retardant containers fitted below turret ring height. 6,800 rounds 7.62mm and 388 rounds of 0.5in for ranging machine gun
Local protection: two multi-barrelled smoke grenade dischargers mounted on turret, fired from under armour

Dimensions

Length: gun forward 10.85m (35ft 7in); gun rear 9.87m (32ft 5in); hull only 7.51m (24ft 89in)
Height: top of cupola 2.82m (9ft 3in)
Width: overall including searchlight 3.62m (11ft 10in); over skirting plates; 3.47m (11ft 6in); over tracks 3.33m (10ft 11in)
Tracks: approach angle 34deg; departure angle 31deg
Nominal ground pressure: 88.29kN/m² 12.8lbf/in²)
Turret ring diameter: 2.15m (7ft 1in)
Ground clearance: 0.51m (1ft 8in)

Automotive performance

Road speed: up to approx 48km/h (30mph)

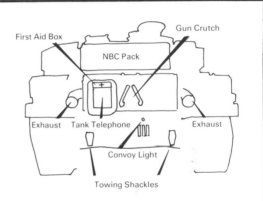

Cross-country speed: 32km/h (20mph)
Vertical obstacle: 0.9m (2ft 11.5in)
Maximum gradient: 35deg (at full tractive effort) (1:4)
Trench crossing: 3.1m (10ft 4in)
Shallow fording: 1.07m (3ft 6in)
Range of action, on road: 400km (250 miles) to 500km (310 miles) on diesel fuel
Power-weight ratio: 13.7 gross bhp (SAE)/long ton

Sighting and vision

Commander's cupola: 1 sight periscopic AFV No 37 Mk 4; 9 periscopes AFV No 40 Mk 2; 1 collimator AFV No 13 or No 18 for laser sight

Overleaf, left: Gunnery practice on the ranges. / *Robin Adshead*

Overleaf, right: A Chieftain, with its 120mm gun in the travel position, speeds along a German road. / *Robin Adshead*

Gunner: 1 sight periscopic, AFV No 59 Mk 1 or tank laser sight No 3 Mk 1 and muzzle reference system (to check sight/bore alignment); 1 sight unit, AFV No 70 or 80 Mk 1 (telescopic); 1 quadrant fire control AFV No 14 Mk 1
Loader: 1 periscope, AFV No 30 Mk 1 (1,220mil × 1 direct vision)
Driver: 1 periscope, AFV No 36 Mk 1 (wide angle direct vision)

Night fighting equipment

Main searchlight aligned with armament to provide white or infra-red light
Commander's white/infra-red spotlight aligned with the cupola machine gun
Two white and two infra-red driving headlights
Sights: infra-red periscope L1A1 for commander and infra-red periscope L4A1 for gunner
Driver: image-intensifying periscope

Gun control system

Manual and electric at the gunner's position and electric at the commander's position
Turret stabilised in azimuth and gun mounting in elevation, to provide stabilised power lay for gunner and commander with vehicle on the move
Commander's over-ride on power controls only
Provision for automatic line-up of turret and commander's cupola
Emergency power traverse provided direct from vehicle batteries
Range finding by ranging machine gun and/or tank laser sight

Protection

Ventilation and nuclear, biological and chemical filter system
Infra-red detector on turret roof

Engines

Main: L60 Mk 8A six-cylinder opposed-piston two-stroke, output 750bhp gross at 2,250rev/min; electric and hydraulic starter motors
Auxiliary: H30 Mk 10A three-cylinder opposed-piston two-stroke, max output 37bhp gross at 3,000rev/min

Transmission

Gearbox: TN12 Merritt-Wilson
Clutch: centrifugal
Steering: Merritt regenerative
Steering brakes: disc hydraulically actuated
Main brakes: disc for foot brake; band for parking brake
Final drive: single spur
Final drive reduction ratio: 5:1

Controls

Gear change: electro-hydraulic
Hand brake: mechanical
Foot-brake: hydraulic — power assisted
Steering: hydraulic, with mechanical interlock
Accelerator: mechanical

Suspension

Springs: helical — horizontal
Wheel deflection: bump 159mm (6.25in) (one wheel rising); rebound 82.5mm (3.25in)
Road wheels: 12 pairs of twin wheels in six bogies 127mm (5in) × 792mm (31in) dia
Tracks: dry pin, rubber-padded 609.6mm (24in) wide
Weight of tracks: 4,719kg (10,400lb) per vehicle set
Links per track: 96 (new)
Track pitch: 157mm (6.18in) (new)
Sprocket: 12 teeth, twin ring 610mm (24in) outside diameter

Communications

Radio equipment: Clansman radios and harness or to customer's requirements
Intercommunication: for all crew
Remote control: 185m (200yd) cable reel No 1
Infantry telephone: on rear of hull
The basic vehicle is equipped to accept field conversion kits in both command and control roles, this is for three- and two-set installations

Electric system

28.5kV (24V nominal) dc
Two dc generators, 150A continuously rated output above 1,000rev/min on main engine, 350A continuously rated output on auxiliary engine, with parallel operation and load sharing
Single-phase 267Hz 200V 1.5kVa 0.98 power factor of output provided on auxiliary engine generation for battery heating in addition to dc output
200Ah batteries provided in hull for engine starting and general electrical services. In addition 100Ah batteries provided in turret for radio loads (giving 8h silent watch for basic installation) and emergency power supply for fighting equipment
All hull wiring is double-pole insulated return to prevent radio interference due to currents through the turret race
Batteries: 4 × 12V in series/parallel in hull; 2 × 12V in series in turret

Fire fighting equipment

Detection and warning system: firewire routed throughout engine compartment
Fixed fire fighting system: two BCF bottles to discharge into engine compartment with both internal and external operating handles
Portable equipment: five BCF hand fire extinguishers

5. Firepower

The most important characteristics of any main battle tank are firepower, protection and mobility. Although the major tank producing nations of the world would argue about the order of priority to give to protection and mobility, there is never any argument about the pre-eminence of firepower. The late Field Marshal Montgomery once described the tank as a way of carrying firepower about on the battlefield and clearly the tank's main armament is its *raison d'être*. First and foremost this firepower must be able to destroy enemy tanks quickly and accurately, by day or by night, in all types of weather, at long or short ranges, in any terrain, whether the target and/or the firing vehicle is stationary or on the move. The tank that can do this with its first round will clearly win any engagement.

However, although it is a tank's prime responsibility to deal with enemy tanks, such a complex and expensive weapon system must be able to perform many other tasks if it is to earn its keep. These include being able to deal with the multiplicity of targets found on the modern battlefield, for example, the infantry soldier on his feet, or in his slit trench or his APC (Armoured Personnel Carrier). The tank must be able to deal also with the armed or the reconnaissance helicopter, or the wide variety of soft skinned, partly armoured or fully armoured vehicles which now abound in any mechanised army. This means that the tank must carry a variety of ammunition for its main gun, plus other secondary weapons. How many and of what type, varies with the tank design and the degree of priority the customer allots to these other roles.

In this chapter I want to look at the whole gamut of weapons carried by Chieftain, and at the complex gun control equipment (including the latest computer controlled IFCS), the observation, sighting, laying and firing gear that goes into this highly sophisticated AFV.

THE MAIN GUN

Despite the reputation of the British 105mm tank gun, which is in service all over the world — for example, it is mounted on the American M60A1, the German Leopard Standardpanzer, the Swedish Strv103, the Swiss Pz61 and Pz68, the Vickers tank (known as the Vijayanta in the Indian army), the Japanese STB-1 and, of course, on countless Centurions, despite all this evidence of proven ability, the British tank gun designers went for a larger calibre weapon. They did so only after carefully sifting through all the evidence of what type of tank the Chieftain might find itself having to deal with in a global war which, God forbid, could occur at any time during its expected 25-year lifespan. They chose the 120mm calibre which has meant going for bagged charge ammunition, for reasons which will be obvious to anyone who has loaded a few rounds for the BAT anti-tank gun, which has 120mm fixed ammunition! However, as Les Monger has already pointed out, as well as being easier to handle, this type of ammunition does have many other advantages: it is more economical in stowage space; it saves weight; there is no brass case to be disposed of; and it virtually eliminates fumes in the turret. With a rate of fire comparable to the majority of other tanks (8-10 rounds in the first minute and six rounds/min thereafter) Chieftain's devastating accuracy and lethality more than compensate for the added complexities which the use of separated ammunition inevitably brings.

The gun fires two main types of armour defeating round, although others are being developed. These are Armour Piercing Discarding Sabot (APDS) and High Explosive Squash Head (HESH). APDS is a super velocity round consisting of a very hard tungsten alloy core, surrounded by a softer segmented metal casing of aluminium alloy. This casing is called a Sabot (lit: a 'shoe') and on the projectile leaving the barrel the sabot separates, allowing the hard core to travel on to the target at very high speed, enabling it to punch a hole through the armour plate of all known battle tanks out to all ranges within normal visibility.

Overleaf: A striking front view of the latest prototype of the Shir Mk 2 seen on the test track at MVEE. / *Crown copyright*

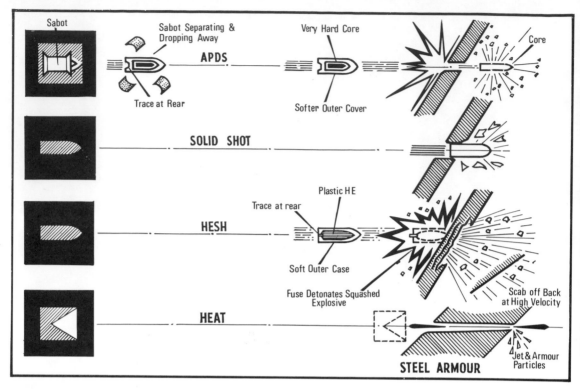

Sabot

Sabot Separating & Dropping Away

Very Hard Core

Core

APDS

Trace at Rear

Softer Outer Cover

SOLID SHOT

Plastic HE

Trace at rear

HESH

Soft Outer Case

Fuse Detonates Squashed Explosive

Scab off Back at High Velocity

HEAT

Jet & Armour Particles

STEEL ARMOUR

HESH is a dual purpose round which can be used as High Explosive, to defeat soft targets, such as infantry in the open or transport, but its main use is against armour. When the projectile hits the enemy tank the outer shell casing collapses, allowing the HE charge inside to squash into a 'pancake' on the outside of the armour. A base fuse then detonates the HE and the shock waves produced by the explosion travel through the armour and cause a large scab of metal to fly off from the inside surface. This hurtles around inside the enemy AFV, causing great damage as it breaks up.

Other types of ammunition include the illuminating, canister and smoke rounds. The latter is filled with white phosphorus and bursts on impact, producing an immediate cloud of dense white smoke. Unlike more conventional base ejection smoke, this cloud does not take long to build up, although it does dissipate more quickly. Consequently, it is more a blinding rather than a screening round. The muzzle velocities and extreme ranges of these rounds are:

	APDS		HESH	Smoke
Muzzle Velocity (m/sec)	1,370		670	670
Extreme Range (m)	3,200		Direct: 3,200	3,200
			Semi-Indirect: 8,000	8,000
			Indirect: 10,600	10,600

To supplement the existing family of rounds the Royal Armament Research and Development Establishment at Fort Halstead, is developing additional rounds and improving in-service rounds so that the capability of the Chieftain may further be improved. The performance of these new rounds is still classified, but the new system is expected to maintain Chieftain's position as the most powerful gun for many years to come.

The 120mm L11 gun consists of the following main components:

The *barrel*, a single tube forging, autofrettaged, with a rifled bore and a chamber at the rear end.

A *fume extractor* is fitted about one third of the way down its length and it is covered with a *thermal sleeve* to protect it when hot during firing in bad weather conditions, because a barrel as long as that of the 120mm will distort in cold wind or rain with consequent loss of accuracy.

The *breech ring* is rectangular in shape with a vertically sliding breech block. The ring is secured to the barrel by interrupted threads and a locking plate.

The *yoke*, which is the means by which the gun is attached to the recoil mechanism, is secured to the breech ring.

The final component is the *breech mechanism* to open and close the breech.

Far left: Fig 6 Effects of anti-tank ammunition on steel armour.

Left: 120mm HESH and APDS projectiles and bag charges, together with their inner and outer containers in which the ammo is stored and transported up to the regimental echelon, who unbox it and load it into specially racked Stalwart high mobility load carriers, which replenish the tanks in the combat area. / *Crown copyright*

Overleaf:

Top left: Back view of the Shir Mk 2 prototype at MVEE. / *Crown copyright*

Bottom left: A 3RTR Chieftain negotiates wooded country. / *Soldier*

Right: A Chieftain on exercise. / *Robin Adshead*

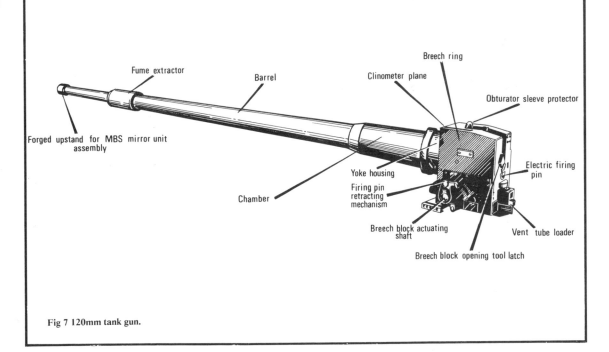

Fig 7 120mm tank gun.

The latest version of the 120mm gun is the L11 A5 model, which incorporates a forged upstand for the mirror of the Muzzle Reference System (MRS) which provides a means whereby the gunner can align his sight with the axis of the muzzle of the gun without dismounting to fit the Muzzle Bore Sight (MBS). The MRS can be used at night and without the need for an aiming mark at 1,100m range. Work is also in progress on an 'Improved Technology Gun', made of Electro Slag Refined (ESR) steel, which is capable of withstanding much greater pressures so that more powerful propellant charges can be used. This gun, also a 120mm with a rifled bore, weighs nearly 2,000kg (1.96 tons) of which over 60% is the weight of the 5.68m (18.74ft) barrel! It is interchangeable with the L11, so could well be fitted into the Chieftain or the Shir at a later date.

Left: Close-up of mirror for MRS. / *Crown copyright*

Below: A Chieftain engages a target at the Warcop Tank Gunnery Range, the gunner is a trainee from the ABTU at Catterick. / *COI*

Right: Gun cleaning in progress at Lulworth Ranges, home of the RAC Gunnery School, where the Royal Armoured Corps train their tank gunnery instructors. / *COI*

Below right: Using a Muzzle Bore Sight to establish the correct relationship between the gun and the sights. / *COI*

Gun Control Equipment

The FV GCE No 7, as fitted to the Chieftain, provides stabilisation to the main gun, with power elevation and traverse controls for the gunner and commander. The turret traverse time for one complete revolution is 18sec. In basic terms the GCE operates by applying gyroscopic control to the gun traverse and elevation axes through a servo loop. This stabilises the gun so that it is unaffected by movement of the hull as the tank manoeuvres at speed or negotiates rough terrain. The principles of the servo system are similar to those employed on Centurion, indeed the GCE No 7 is best described as an uprated version of the well proven FVGCE No 1 as fitted to the Centurion, with those improvements necessary to match the more stringent needs for quicker response times, greater accuracy and the heavier turret. There are four modes of GCE operation: non-stabilised, stabilised, emergency and manual.

Non-Stabilised Mode

With the tank stationary and the equipment in the unstabilised mode, the gunner is part of a fast response servo-system, controlling traverse and elevation, while

Left: This photograph of two Chieftains of the Queen's Royal Irish Hussars on the training area near Paderborn gives a graphic impression of the size of the 120mm main tank gun. / *COI*

Below: Fig 8 Fire control system.

he observes his target through his sights. He has power control through his single duplex controller for traverse and elevation, and can rapidly traverse or elevate in a few seconds, or track a moving target to within less than one minute of arc. The commander has an override duplex controller for both elevation and traverse, so that he can quickly lay the gun on to a new target.

Stabilised Mode

With the tank moving, particularly across rough country, accurate gun laying would normally be impossible. In the stabilised mode a pair of rate gyros, mounted on the gun cradle, produce electrical signals in proportion to the angular velocity in space of the gun in traverse and elevation. These signals are combined with the output from a tachometer-generator to form a 're-set' signal which is then injected into the appropriate servo channel. The effect is to keep the muzzle of the gun pointed at the same point in space. Thus, in a Chieftain moving at speed across rough country, if the gunner now makes only the normal tracking corrections, the gun will continue to point at the target irrespective of the attitude of the vehicle hull.

Emergency Mode

The turret can only be traversed at fixed speeds to the left or right and a stopping position selected.

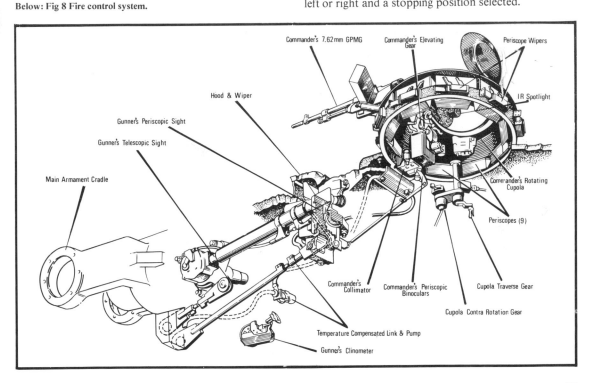

65

Manual Controls

In addition to his power controls, the gunner is provided with a manual control for elevation and a two-speed manual control for traverse. The commander has no manual controls for the main gun, but can of course traverse his cupola by hand and elevate his machine gun. Hand traverse is normally only used for fine laying in static shooting or as a last resort in the event of a total power failure.

The Ranging Machine Gun (RMG)

The RMG is a Browning, calibre .50in (12.7mm), and is matched to the main armament, to enable the gunner to determine the range and azimuth bearing to the target before firing the 120mm. He does this by observing the fall of shot from the RMG as the rounds have both a long burning trace and a flashing compound in the nose, which makes it easier to observe the strike. The gun is a modified version of the .50in M2 HB Browning and is fired electrically. It is automatic, recoil operated, air cooled and belt fed from the left side. It can be fired independently from the electric firing gear and can be set for single shot operation if required. The gun is mounted in a cradle which is adjustable in its relation to the main armament. A tray fixed to the turret adjacent to the RMG holds the ammunition box from which the linked ammunition passes direct into the feedway of the gun. The spent cases and links drop into a chute which carries them into a disposal tube below the gun. The firing gear has a solenoid fitted to the right side of the gun which, when energised, operates the sear. A foot operated plunger switch and a fire controller limit the gun to firing bursts of three rounds for each switch operation. When using the RMG to discover the range to the target, the gunner fires three bursts at pre-determined and ever increasing ranges. The range at which the first burst strikes or goes plus of the target is then transferred to the main gun, by using the graticule pattern on the gunner's sight; he then engages the target with an armour defeating round with the maximum chance of a first round hit. The ammunition for the RMG has recently been improved

to give a range of 2,500m instead of 1,800m. Other data is as follows:

Length: 5ft 5.2in (1,654mm)
Weight: $72\frac{1}{2}$lb (33kg)
Cyclic rate of fire: 400-600rpm
Controlled rate of fire: 240rpm
Feed: 100rd disintegrating belt

Six boxes of .50in ammunition are carried each containing a belt of 100rd. Once the laser rangefinder has been fully tested in all conditions of service, then it is likely that the RMG will be dispensed with.

The Machine Guns

The two 7.62mm General Purpose Machine Guns are used primarily to kill men in the open. The L8A1 was specially designed for use as a coaxial machine gun in the Chieftain. In order to fit it into the restricted space available and to reduce the escape of propellant gases into the turret certain changes had to be made to the gun; it can, however, be quickly converted to the ground (LMG) role by fitting a butt and bipod. The trigger mechanism is fitted with a folding grip for use when firing by hand. The rate of fire is controlled by a three-port gas regulator and with a cold gun and the regulator set in its normal setting (No 2 port) gives a rate of fire of 650-750rpm. The L37A1 has been designed for use either mounted on the commander's cupola or dismounted. Both guns have a similar performance with a muzzle velocity of 2,800ft/sec (850m/sec) and a range of 1,100m (limited by trace burn out). On the tank, 30 boxes of 7.62mm ammunition are carried, with each box containing a belt of 200 rounds, mixed ball and trace.

Extensive trials have resulted in a new design of link exit chute, a lighter more compact feed tray, a new cartridge stop (angled to prevent link jams using any type of link), a new and stronger feed arm and an improved breech block roller. These improvements

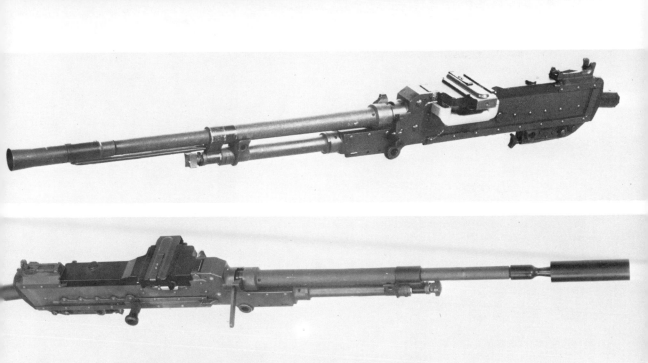

Top: The L8A1 7.62mm General Purpose Machine Gun, specially designed for use as the 'coax' for Chieftain. / *Crown copyright*

Above: The L8A2 improved model of the GPMG which is superior to the vast majority of other coax machine guns in the world. / *Crown copyright*

Left: A young commander of the 4/7RDG loads his commander's GPMG with a new belt of ammunition. / *Crown copyright*

have all been incorporated into the L8A2 model, which will be the coax for the Shir, and its counterpart, the FN MAG 38, which has been chosen by both the USA and Canada as their new coaxial tank machine gun (trials in the USA found that the GPMG was superior to any other comparable weapon in the vehicle role).

The Smoke Grenade Dischargers

The smoke grenade dischargers are used to provide a quick local smokescreen when the tank is caught out in the open and needs a breathing space to dive for cover. One Discharger No 9 is fitted on each side of the turret, containing six discharger cups in a single casting. The grenades are electrically fired from inside the tank by the tank commander. They are projected about 60m over a lateral spread of some 1,800mil. The resulting screen builds up immediately because the grenades are white phosphorus, and quickly hides the tank.

Vison Devices

The Barr & Stroud Tank Laser Range-finder system (Tank Laser Sight No 1 Mk 2 [TLS]) was developed under a Ministry of Defence contract as the standard gunner's laser sight for Chieftain. The sight houses the laser transmitter, the receiver system and the optical sight. The line of sight in elevation is aligned to the axis of the gun by means of a precision parallel linkage, and in azimuth by coincident turret mounting. Boresighting of the TLS is achieved using controls on the unit in conjunction with either the MBS or the MRS. Gun laying is achieved through a ballistic graticule. Laser ranging can be initiated by the gunner or remotely by the commander. The range is displayed in the left eyepiece of the TLS and remotely at the commander's station on the commander's Range Read-Out Unit. When a target is partially obscured by smoke or other obstacles the selection of 'last range' on the ranging unit allows the true range to be obtained by eliminating all received echoes other than the last echo, which comes from the target. TLS has the inbuilt capability to accept a conversion kit which provides a projected graticule aiming mark when it is used integrated within IFCS.

Specification

Sighting telescope is a ×10 magnification; system can operate from 500 to 10,000m with an accuracy of ± 20m max error (± 10m for 90% of shots); firing rate is 10 shots/min with a burst capability of three shots in 4sec, capacitor charging time is 2sec.

Right: The Commander's sight AV No 37, showing the eyepieces, the sight gives either ×1 or ×10 magnification. Above is the Commander's cupola service switch box. / *MSDS Stanmore*

Left: IFCS, the Tank Laser Sight No 1 Mark 2. Note the 'laser flash' button bottom left, just below the total flash counter. On the rear of the sight body is the ×1 window (with blackout shutter) and below it two eyepieces. The RH is the ×8×10 eyepiece, whilst the one on the left enables the gunner to see the lased range readout in figures. / *Barr & Stroud Ltd*

Right: The view through the TLS right hand eyepiece, showing part of the graticule pattern, with the ballistic aiming mark circling the target. / *MSDS Stanmore*

Below: Close-up of the No 21 cupola, showing the heads of the Image Intensifier night sight (on left) and the thermal pointer (on right). / *Crown copyright*

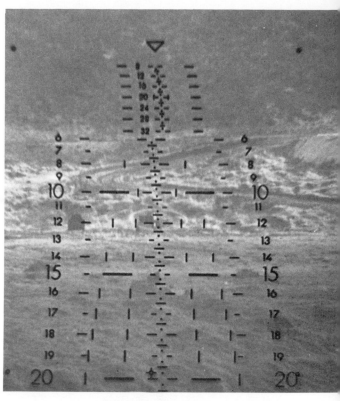

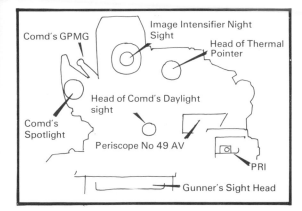

Above: IFCS, external view of Chieftain showing the meteorological probe in its protective grid. / *MSDS Stanmore*

Left: A good view of the IR detector on its stalk just behind the commander's cupola. (The larger light on the LHS of the tank is part of the Simfire equipment — see Chapter 13.) / *Crown copyright*

IFCS — the Fully Integrated Fire Control System

Success and survival in a tank battle depends on fire supremacy. A tank that can fire the first round of any engagement in the minimum time with the maximum accuracy, has its combat effectiveness and chance of survival immeasurably enhanced. Developed by Marconi Space and Defence Systems Ltd for Chieftain, the fully integrated fire control system provides a higher degree of accuracy and a much shorter response time than any other tank fire control system in the world today. The primary task of IFCS is to solve the direct fire engagement problem for both main and secondary armaments and for all types of ammunition in service.

The success of IFCS depends upon the close integration of four main elements — a computer based data handling sub-system, a laser sight, a sensor sub-system and the gun control equipment. In Chieftain this integration gives the tank a battle superiority second to none, and exploits the full potential of the 120mm gun. IFCS is automatic and extremely rapid in operation. In just over three seconds of laying on the

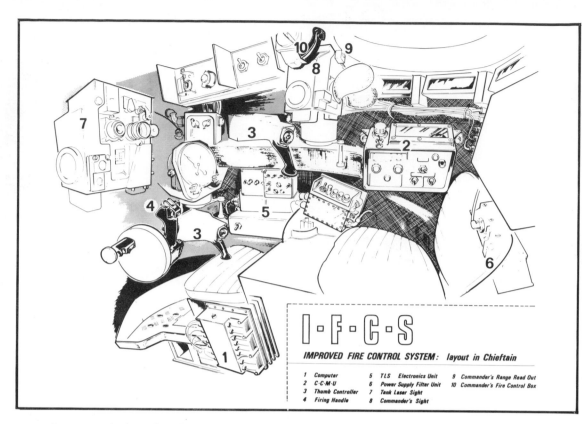

I·F·C·S

IMPROVED FIRE CONTROL SYSTEM: layout in Chieftain

1	Computer	5	TLS Electronics Unit	9	Commander's Range Read Out
2	C·C·M·U	6	Power Supply Filter Unit	10	Commander's Fire Control Box
3	Thumb Controller	7	Tank Laser Sight		
4	Firing Handle	8	Commander's Sight		

target, the gun can be brought to bear, with the correct aim-off applied, and fired with a strong certainty of obtaining a first round hit. This is equally true for a moving target, or for a moving own vehicle, or both, and applies out to the full effective range of the tank's main armament. Secondary tasks of the system include computations for semi-indirect and indirect fire and corrections to fire using HESH ammunition from a stationary tank at extended ranges. IFCS is designed for simplicity of operation and high reliability. The equipment is rugged enough to withstand extremes of climate and military environment. It will therefore perform within specifications under all conditions.

The superiority of IFCS lies in the fact that the system can almost think for itself. The brain of the system, the Marconi 12-12P digital computer, is programmed for the specific armaments and ammunition carried by the tank and gathers information from a number of sensors. These sensors are located about the tank and form one of the four sub-systems. The computer, having been told the armament and ammunition to be used against a particular target, accepts range from the sighting sub-system, absorbs the meteorological and other gun position data from the sensors, calculates the future position of the target

Above: Fig 9 IFCS — layout in Chieftain.

Above right: Fig 10 IFCS — main components.

Right: Fig 11 IFCS — operating sequence.

and, via the gun control equipment, automatically lays the gun on the correct line and angle for the ammunition in use. All that happens in a matter of seconds.

The diagrams which accompany this chapter show: the layout of IFCS in a Chieftain turret; the main components in schematic layout; the operating sequence and, finally, a typical direct fire engagement for a crossing target. The procedure for the last of these is also outlined below. It is a gunner's shoot but the commander has a priority override and can take personal control at any time.

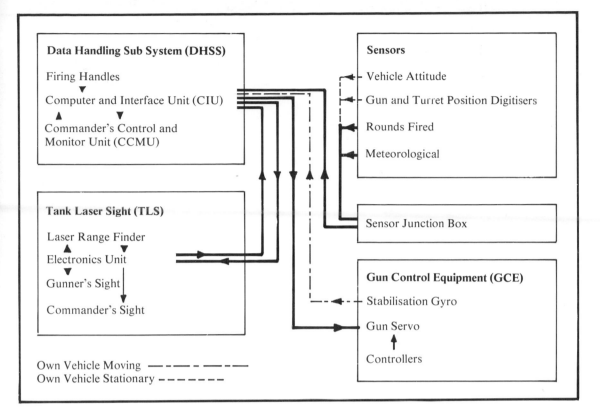

Data Handling Sub System (DHSS)

Firing Handles
▼
Computer and Interface Unit (CIU)
▲   ▼
Commander's Control and
Monitor Unit (CCMU)

Tank Laser Sight (TLS)

Laser Range Finder
▲   ▼
Electronics Unit
▼
Gunner's Sight

Commander's Sight

Own Vehicle Moving — · — · — · —
Own Vehicle Stationary — — — — — —

Sensors

Vehicle Attitude

Gun and Turret Position Digitisers

Rounds Fired

Meteorological

Sensor Junction Box

Gun Control Equipment (GCE)

Stabilisation Gyro

Gun Servo
▲
Controllers

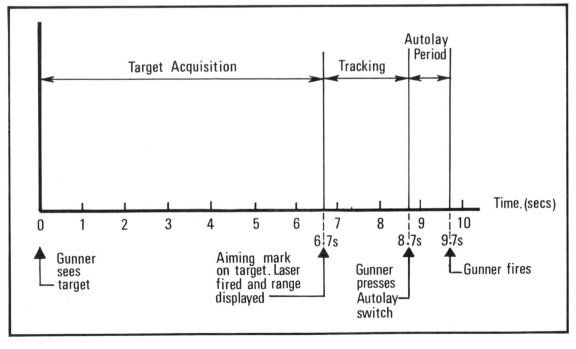

Target Acquisition

Tracking

Autolay
Period

Time. (secs)

0   1   2   3   4   5   6   7   8   9   10

6.7s   8.7s   9.7s

Gunner
sees
target

Aiming mark
on target. Laser
fired and range
displayed

Gunner
presses
Autolay
switch

Gunner fires

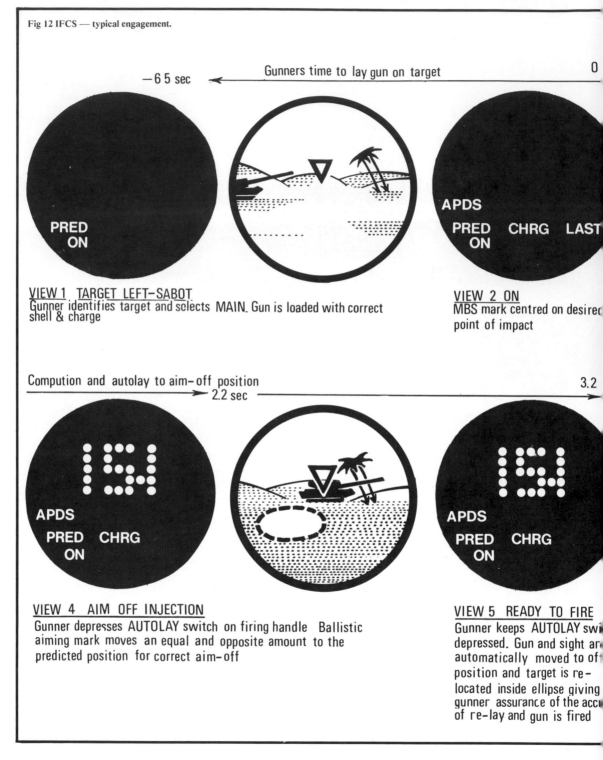

Fig 12 IFCS — typical engagement.

Gunners time to lay gun on target

−6 5 sec ←

0

PRED
ON

VIEW 1 TARGET LEFT−SABOT
Gunner identifies target and selects MAIN. Gun is loaded with correct shell & charge

APDS
PRED   CHRG   LAST
ON

VIEW 2 ON
MBS mark centred on desired point of impact

Computation and autolay to aim−off position

2.2 sec

3.2

APDS
PRED   CHRG
ON

VIEW 4   AIM OFF INJECTION
Gunner depresses AUTOLAY switch on firing handle Ballistic aiming mark moves an equal and opposite amount to the predicted position for correct aim−off

APDS
PRED   CHRG
ON

VIEW 5   READY TO FIRE
Gunner keeps AUTOLAY swi depressed. Gun and sight ar automatically moved to off position and target is re- located inside ellipse giving gunner assurance of the accu of re-lay and gun is fired

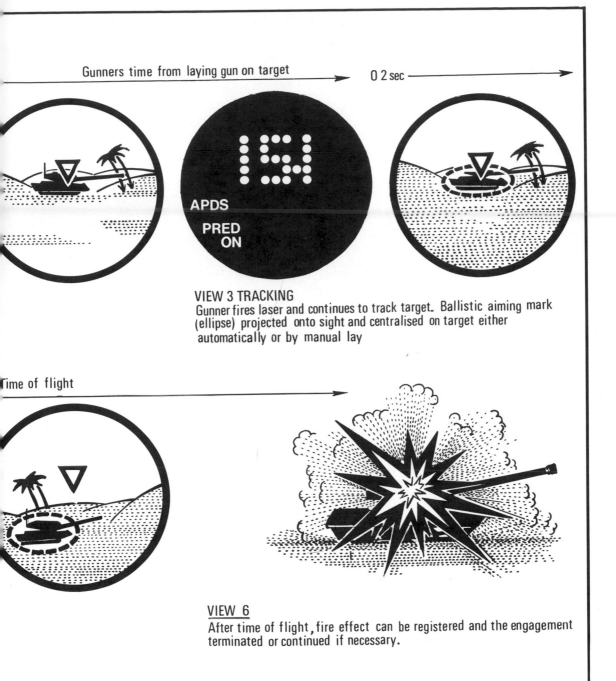

Gunners time from laying gun on target

0 2 sec

Time of flight

VIEW 3 TRACKING
Gunner fires laser and continues to track target. Ballistic aiming mark
(ellipse) projected onto sight and centralised on target either
automatically or by manual lay

APDS
PRED
ON

VIEW 6
After time of flight, fire effect can be registered and the engagement
terminated or continued if necessary.

View 1. A target is observed and on the order 'TARGET LEFT — SABOT', the gunner puts his armament switch to *Main*. The computer automatically selects APDS (other types of ammo have to be selected by a Select button on the firing handle), and the laser is charged. The sequence is shown on the commander's remote and gunner's displays. The loader loads the correct shell and associated charge.

View 2. Using his thumb controller the gunner brings the desired point of impact on the target to coincide with the MBS mark on the graticule, reports 'ON' and commences tracking — ie maintains coincidence between MBS and target, using his thumb controller.

View 3. When the gunner has commenced tracking by maintaining coincidence between the target and the MBS mark, he fires the laser and continues to track thereby feeding the computer with rates of elevation and traverse. Laser range is automatically transmitted to the computer and almost instantly the ballistic aiming mark is projected on to the TLS with the ellipse circumscribing the target and its centre coincident with the MBS mark.

View 4. When satisfied that the size of the ellipse gives a correct indication of range, the gunner depresses the *Autolay* switch on the firing handle: the ballistic aiming mark moves inversely to the predicted position for a correct aim-off for the weapon and ammunition selected.

View 5. The gunner keeps the *Autolay* switch depressed and, as the sight is linked to the gun, the gun moves to the offset position bringing the target once again into coincidence with the ballistic aiming mark ellipse, where it remains under automatic control. This gives the gunner assurance to fire the gun with accuracy. (Whilst *Autolay* is pressed the computer takes over control of the tracking from the thumb controller. If the gunner's initial lay or tracking was inaccurate, causing the ellipse (after *Autolay*) not to coincide with the target, the *Autolay* switch can be released and a fine lay made by means of the thumb controller to bring the aiming mark on to the target.)

View 6. During the flight of the shell, the target and ellipse are still automatically retained. After observation of fire effect the engagement can either be continued or terminated.

This page: A sequence showing the operation of the tank searchlight (Light Projector No 2 Mk 3). The first (bottom left) shows the searchlight with the outer door closed. The outer case assembly is of welded steel and contains a cooling fan motor — approx weight of complete assembly is 500lb. Next photo (left) shows the SL with armoured door open and IR door in place. Final shot (below) is with both doors open, showing the 19in diameter parabolic mirror and the Xenon lamp. The control box is in the turret for the commander's use. It has a four position switch (OFF – standby – IR – WH ie white light); also a singleboost switch which will temporarily increase power from 2kW to 3kW (for not more than 10sec at a time). / *Crown copyright*

Overleaf: A dramatic line up of Chieftains all using their searchlights. / *Crown copyright*

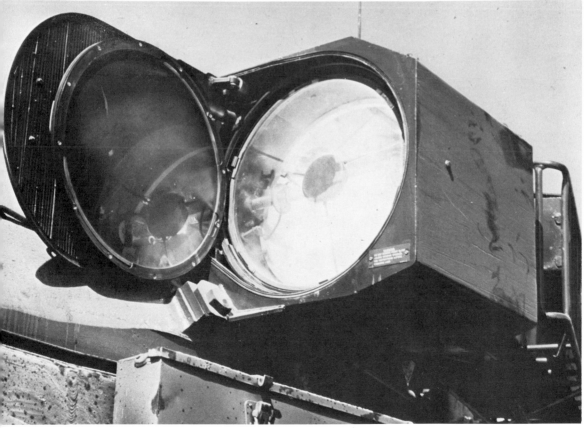

6. Protection

Protection is vital because it allows the tank to move about on the battlefield with its crew, gun and engine all relatively safe from enemy fire. There are a number of ways in which a tank can protect itself — for example, by having a high cross-country speed or a low silhouette, by the intelligent use of ground or by camouflage. However, the most important primary means of protection is the armour plate from which the tank is built. In line with current UK policy the Chieftain tank mainly depends upon the thickness of its armour for protection, rather than upon increased speed or agility, although it is certainly no slouch. The last two Middle East wars have vindicated the British philosophy, in that the most successful tank was undoubtedly the adequately armoured Centurion, rather than the lighter, faster T55 and T62. As Chieftain is likely to have to fight its battles out numbered and on the defensive, it must be capable of living on the battlefield for long periods and of absorbing punishment while dealing effectively with the enemy tanks which do not have its immunity. Mobility was therefore put at a slightly lower priority than protection in the original design. With its excellent frontal armour and good all round protection Chieftain must be the best protected modern AFV. It has a high level of immunity from mines by virtue of its sloping hull sides, whilst the combination of skirting plates with track and suspension, gives a good protection against infantry hollow charge weapons.

Chobham Armour

Recent British developments in the field of protection will ensure that Chieftain's derivative the Shir 2 and Chieftain's successor in the British Army, will be even better protected. These developments are centred on a new type of armour known as 'Chobham' armour, after its MVEE birthplace.

Below: Chobham armour on an experimental tank. This AFV was designed and developed at the Military Vehicles and Engineering Establishment (MVEE) at Chobham. Photograph taken June 1976. / Crown copyright

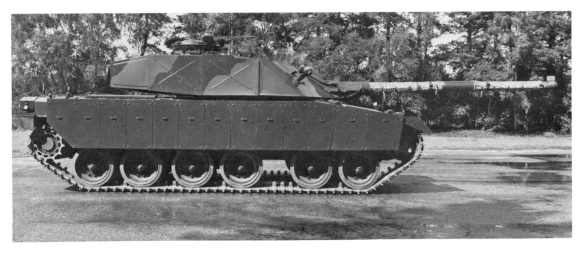

Above: Chobham armour on an experimental tank. Chobham armour provides unprecedented protection against all forms of attack and was described by the last Secretary of State for Defence as 'the most significant achievement in tank design and protection since World War II'. / *Crown copyright*

NBC Protection

To survive on the modern battlefield a tank requires the ability to protect its crew from nuclear fall out, bacteriological or chemical attacks. Ideally this means being able to seal off the inside of the AFV and then provide a supply of clean, filtered air to the crew, so that they do not need to wear special clothing or respirators which degrade their performance. Chieftain achieves this protection through an NBC/ventilation pack, which is mounted on the inside of an armoured box attached to the rear of the turret. The pack has four filtration stages, a cyclone separator, a two-layer synthetic fibre pre-filter, an ultra high efficiency glass fibre paper particulate filter and a battery of four cylindrical anti-vapour filters, containing chemically activated charcoal and resin impregnated wool. There are two fans, one to circulate the air for normal ventilation purposes, the other for NBC conditions. Air is drawn through all four stages of filtration under NBC conditions, but only through the first two for normal ventilation. The filtered air is then ducted inside the tank to a series of diffusers located beside crew positions. Each diffuser has a respirator adaptor and a blanking plate. The environmental conditions created by the ventilation and filtration system and NBC pack, together with an adequate supply of electric power and of drinking water, enable the crew to remain fully effective when closed down for 48 hours at a stretch.

On 17 June 1976, the Secretary of State for Defence announced the development of a completely new type of armour in the UK. He said that it represented the most significant achievement in tank design since World War II. It provides a high level of protection against all forms of attack, including the HEAT anti-tank warhead favoured for guided weapons. Weight for weight it gives better protection than *any* other type of existing armour against *all* forms of anti-tank weapons. Chobham armour is to be fitted on the Shir Mark 2 derivative of Chieftain, but currently there are no plans to fit it on to the existing British Army Chieftains, although it will clearly be a must for MBT 80.

Above and left: On the battlefield,
protection is not purely a matter of
heavier armour or faster speed than
one's opponent. Tactical fire
positions and the use of natural
camouflage are essential
components in the art of protection.
/ *Crown copyright*

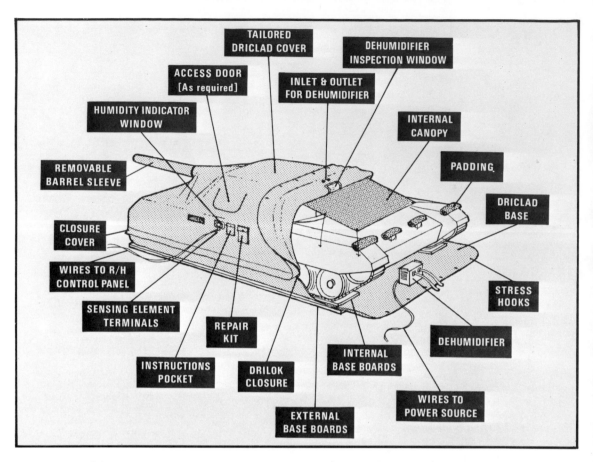

TAILORED
DRICLAD COVER

DEHUMIDIFIER
INSPECTION WINDOW

ACCESS DOOR
[As required]

INLET & OUTLET
FOR DEHUMIDIFIER

HUMIDITY INDICATOR
WINDOW

INTERNAL
CANOPY

REMOVABLE
BARREL SLEEVE

PADDING

DRICLAD
BASE

CLOSURE
COVER

WIRES TO R/H
CONTROL PANEL

STRESS
HOOKS

SENSING ELEMENT
TERMINALS

REPAIR
KIT

DEHUMIDIFIER

INSTRUCTIONS
POCKET

DRILOK
CLOSURE

INTERNAL
BASE BOARDS

WIRES TO
POWER SOURCE

EXTERNAL
BASE BOARDS

Driclad Protection

In line with other modern AFVs, Chieftain is designed
and built to very high standards so that it can withstand all types of climate and conditions all over the
world. However, no AFV has yet been built which will
not suffer damage from corrosion, fungal bloom,
insects etc, particularly when the vehicle has to be left
virtually unattended for long periods of time. Such a
situation applies to AFVs in storage or held as part of
a unit's war reserve. They must, with the minimum of
maintenance and inspection, remain viable and ready
at any moment to be taken into service.

Such protection is given by the Driclad System
which was taken into approved British Army service
in 1965, after exhaustive tropical trials lasting for two
years in the humid climate of South East Asia. Since
then it has been used successfully all over the world.
The trials results exceeded all expectations, even in the
most humid conditions of the hot open site, very close
to the jungle, with salt-laden sea air as an added
hazard. It was conclusively proved that the vehicles
could be stored ready for action and in complete

Above: Fig 13 The Driclad system. / Driclad Ltd

safety. Even optical instruments were absolutely free
from fungal bloom after two years' outdoor storage.
When required for use the tanks started up at the
touch of a switch without any action apart from the
removal of the Driclad covers and the connection of
the vehicle batteries.

The system is based on the enclosure of the tank in
a flexible specially formulated plastic cover. The cover
is sealed by an easy to open closure strip, which is
moisture vapour-proof. Humidity inside the cover is
controlled either by a mechanical dehumidifier or by
desiccant in special containers which can be dried out
for reuse by a heater fan in the carrier. The significant
advantages of this system are: reliability of equipment
stored for immediate use; no elaborate preparation for
storage needed; long life of the re-usable covers which
can be installed, supervised and repaired by unskilled
operators; covers permit access for inspection during
storage.

7. Mobility

It is very seldom that a tank has a need to use really high road speeds. Battlefield tactical mobility is a far more valuable asset, to enable the tank to get about the battlefield at a reasonable speed and to move agilely from one fire position to another. In Chieftain the provision of this type of mobility has been the main consideration and the continual uprating of the main engine has been to achieve this agility rather than a high top speed.

The Leyland L60 Engine

'The performance of the Chieftain's gun and range finding equipment is first class. It is therefore all the more unsatisfactory that the tank should have been let down by its engine in the past'. So wrote the House of Commons Defence and Technical Affairs Sub-Committee, in the conclusion to their report on the Chieftain tank engine, published on 23 May 1978. I do not intend to recount in detail the complete unhappy saga of the Leyland L60 engine, which has for so long bedevilled Chieftain. However, it would be wrong not to mention at least some of the problems and to see what has been and still is being done to rectify them. From the outset the development of the engine was rushed and the then UK policy to go for multi-fuel capability added greatly to its complexity.

There have been four main areas of engine failure namely: cracking of the cylinder liners, failure of the cylinder lip seals, piston fire ring breakages and, finally, cracking of rear gear cases. Good progress has already been made in curing at least some of these problems, such as the liner cracking and the piston ring breakages. Liners made from improved material, with better thermal and wear properties, together with a new design of piston rings, have been introduced, with much success. Modifications to the fan drive in order to prevent high stresses being applied to the rear

Below: The Chieftain power pack. / *Simon Dunstan*

gear cases are being introduced and are proving successful. An improved method of sealing between the liners and the cylinder block has also been tried. The method is known as 'tight fit' and involves an interference fit between the liner and block. Provided all trials continue to go according to plan it is intended to introduce 'tight fit liner build' standard to all L60 engines in two phases: first a number of new engines, originally ordered as spares, will be fitted with tight fit liners and then introduced into the overhaul line. If they are successful, then all Chieftains will be fitted with the modified engines in a major overhaul programme. These engines will not only embody tight fit liners, plus all the other improvements mentioned above, but will also have a number of other power pack modifications. Collectively these should make a considerable improvement to the reliability of the engine. To date there is no intention to fit British Army Chieftains with the new Rolls-Royce CV12 engine described below.

The Rolls-Royce CV12TCA Engine

The Shir derivatives of Chieftain will be powered by an entirely new power pack, the Rolls-Royce CV12TCA diesel engine, one of a series of new vee-engines being made by the recently formed Military Engine Division

of Rolls-Royce, in their spanking new factory at Shrewsbury. Rolls-Royce have been closely associated with military vehicles for almost 60 years and, during World War II, their famous Meteor engine powered the Cromwell, Challenger and Comet tanks and was also specified for the postwar Centurion. Their multi-fuel K60 engine currently powers the British FV430 series of armoured tracked vehicles and the Swedish S tank. The design concept behind this new family of engines springs from a relaxation in the strict requirements of multi-fuel capability for AFV engines, which was only achieved, as we have seen with the L60 engine, at the expense of considerable design complexity. The new series are of a straightforward, orthodox design, capable of withstanding rough treatment, because no light alloys have been used in the main engine structure. Lightness has been achieved by concentrating upon extreme compactness of design, whilst the four-stroke cycle together with open combustion chambers have been adopted so as to minimise thermal problems normally associated with high output engines. The CV12 has a 60° Vee angle for consideration of low crankshaft stresses and minimum engine width. The aim has been to produce an extremely reliable, economical engine with long service life between overhauls.

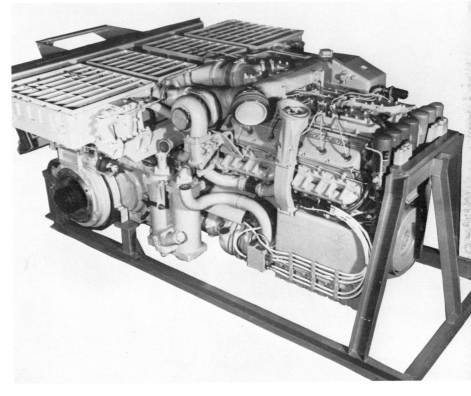

Left: Close up of an L60 engine being worked on by a REME mechanic of the LAD 17th/21st Lancers. / Crown copyright

Right: The Rolls-Royce 1,200hp CV12 TCA power pack which will be fitted into the Shir. / Rolls-Royce

Engine

Type: Direct injection, liquid cooled, four stroke, turbo charged, charge cooled compression ignition
Number of cylinders: 12
Arrangement: 60° included angle Vee
Fuel: Diesel fuel specified in Defence Guide DG-12A and AVTUR for very low ambient temperature operation
Maximum power: 895kW (1,200bhp) at 2,300rpm to BS AU141a test conditions
Direction of rotation: Anti-clockwise viewed on flywheel
Bore: 135mm (5.315in)
Stroke: 152mm (5.984in)
Capacity (Total swept volume): 26.11 litres (1,59.24cu in)
Idling speed: 500-600rpm
Aspiration: Pressure charged by turbochargers
Compression ratio: 12:1 (nominal)
Valve tappet clearance: Inlet 0.4mm (0.016in) hot or cold
Exhaust 0.7mm (0.028in) hot or cold
Fuel injection pump: 12 element, in line, base mounted Maximec MX1212
Fuel feed pressure: 210 to 275kN/sq m (30 to 40lbf/sq in)
Injectors: Axial feed low spring type
Injector valve opening: 24,300kN/sq m (3,528lbf/sq in — 240 atmospheres)
Injector nozzles: 6 hole — 150° included angle spray
Firing order: A1, B6, A4, B3, A2, B5, A6, B1, A3, B4, A5, B2
Valve timing:
Inlet valve open 15.8° BTDC
Inlet valve closed 21.5° ABDC
Exhaust valve open 43.4° BBDC
Exhaust valve closed 17.0° ATDC
Injection timing: 18° BTDC (Static) with ATD
23° BTDC (Static) without ATD

Fuel system

Type: Pressurised; feeding into injection pump gallery and manifold air heater with through flows to base tank
Fuel feed pumps: Base tank mounted in vehicle

Above left: A good view of the FPT Industries Hycatrol flexible fuel tank being checked before fitting into a Chieftain. / *FPT Industries*

Left: Driver maintenance. Track 'bashing' is hard but essential work, as a worn or slack track can spell disaster. / *Crown copyright*

Fuel filters: 3 spin-on type expendable cannisters; engine mounted

Lubrication system

Type: Dry sump
Capacity: 52 litres (11.44 imperial gallons) to *full* mark on dipstick
Oil pump: Three tier gear type
Oil pressure: 415kN/sq m (60lbf/sq in) hot at 2,300rpm
Heat exchanger: Twin, baffled and finned, shell and tube
Oil flow rate: 300 litres/min (66 imperial gallons/min)
Pressure drop: 124kN/sq m (18lbf/sq in)
Filters: 4 spin-on type expendable cannisters
Lubrication oil temperature: Normal 70°C to 100°C (158°F to 212°F)
Maximum 120°C (248°F)

Cooling system

Capacity — Engine: 81 litres (18 imperial gallons)
Capacity — Total: 205 litres (45 imperial gallons)
Coolant flow: 350 litres/min (77 imperial gallons/min) around each bank of cylinders
Radiators: (2) Marston Superpak 3M, 2 × 4 row, 5 fins/cm (13 fins/in), corrugated fin and tube, 0.37sq m (4.0sq ft) counter-cross flow
Charge coolers: (2) Marston plate and fin 0.185sq m (2sq ft) cross flow
Pump: Conventional rotary pump, gear driven; output 700 litres/min (154 imperial gallons/min)
Coolant pressure: Up to 70kN/sq m (10lbf/sq in)
Thermostats: (2) Western Thomson Controls; wax element — quick response 1 off per bank
Cracking: 68°C to 73°C (154°F to 163°F)
Full open: 79°C to 84°C (174°F to 183°F)
Fans: (3) Airscrew Howden 380 MF (380mm diam, mixed flow) driven at 2.4 × engine speed)

Crossing Water Obstacles

A large proportion of water obstacles in North West Europe are less than 22.8m (74.8ft) and thus within the capabilities of the No 8 Scissors type tank bridge as carried by the Chieftain AVLB. However, if tanks are to retain their tactical mobility then they must be able to cross all types of water obstacles, no matter how wide or how deep these may be. The current UK policy is to use engineer bridging or rafting equipment, as the photographs at the beginning of this section show. However, when fitted with schnorkel equipment Chieftain has the ability to deep wade across some water obstacles of suitable depth, and again I have included photos of this method being used. Schnorkelling equipment, which has been proved as being successful on Chieftain, is not in general issue, but could be used if required.

Top right: Chieftain can ford minor water obstacles up to a depth of 1.07m (3ft 6in) without any preparation as this photo of a Blues and Royals Chieftain shows. / *COI*

Centre right: A partly camouflaged Chieftain of the Blues and Royals leaves an M2 heavy floating pontoon bridge across the River Weser, during Exercise Mizzen Mast. / *Crown copyright*

Below: A Chieftain tank belonging to B Squadron, Royal Scots Dragoon Guards, making a heavy ferry crossing of the Havel See in Berlin, under control of 38 (Berlin) Field Squadron. / *Crown copyright*

Left: Chieftain fitted with schnorkel equipment, deep wading across the East Fleet from Chesil Beach to land at Wyke Regis, Dorset. Although current British Army water crossing policy does not include schnorkelling, the Chieftain can be so equipped as this photograph shows. The bed of the river must be firm and obstacle free, whilst the banks must also be firm and not too steep. / Crown copyright

Below: A Chieftain fully equipped for deep wading. The depth for wading depends on various factors, including the height of the tower which can be varied. / Crown copyright

Right: A Chieftain schnorkelIng across the East Fleet, Wyke Regis, Dorset. / *Crown copyright*

Below: Fig 14 Dudley remote control system.

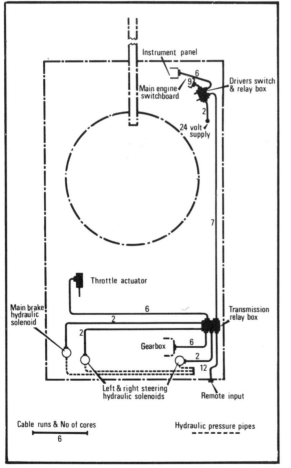

Instrument panel

Main engine switchboard

Drivers switch & relay box

24 volt supply

Throttle actuator

Main brake hydraulic solenoid

Transmission relay box

Gearbox

Left & right steering hydraulic solenoids

Remote input

Cable runs & No of cores

Hydraulic pressure pipes

Remote Control

Major Ken Dudley, late of the Royal Tank Regiment, who is now the head of sales for the Communications Division of Racal Amplivox, was a member of the Equipment Trials Wing, Bovington, in 1968 when he invented a unique method for remotely controlling a Chieftain tank. His equipment could be used for deep wading across water obstacles as the photo shows, and of course in a wide variety of other situations. It makes use of the vehicle 24V supply and the hydraulic pressure system used for the foot brake. The controls are on a remote control box and comprise: on/off switch, starter button, throttle control, tachometer, gear selection, steering and brakes. Transmission between the control box and the tank is by means of a multi-core cable. Within the vehicle the controls are as follows (see diagram):

a Driver's compartment — a small box containing four relays, two switches and two warning lamps. The switches (Remote Control Master switch and Driver's Override switch) are connected with the appropriate warning light on the box. The relays are used for switching on the vehicle and for steering. The Driver's Override also switches the vehicle tachometer sender unit off the vehicle and on to the remote control tachometer.

b Engine compartment — a 24V electro-mechanical actuator is mounted beside the L60 engine and connected to the rack actuating lever. The connections include a lost motion system so that the actuator has no effect on the rack when the AFV is being driven normally.

c Gearbox compartment — a box containing the steering, throttle, braking and gearbox relays is positioned on the right wall of the hull beside the hydraulic oil tank. The gearbox relays are connected directly to the gearbox solenoids. Steering is achieved by applying pressure from the vehicle hydraulic system to the appropriate steering brake. This is done by means of a changeover electro-hydraulic valve on each steering brake. The main brakes are controlled by the third changeover valve. As the hydraulic system used the main hydraulic tank for main brakes and steering, the steering brake hydraulic tank is dispensed with and all oil is drawn from one tank. This does not affect normal driving and reduces the maintenance task from two levels to check to one.

Fail/Safe and mechanical safety is coupled into the circuits in the form of interlocks; for example, should the remote cable break then the engine is automatically switched off and all gears disengaged. This allows a recovery team to attach a cable and pull the tank out of the water. Clearly there are many advantages to the system over normal schnorkelling, a high rigid tower is not required, merely a light

aspiration tube held by nylon guys on a flexible tube with a float. No one is put at risk should the tank hit a mine or flood during crossing. The equipment is much quicker to remove once the AFV has crossed the obstacle. The logistic load for carrying the equipment is considerably reduced. In addition to crossing water obstacles this ingenious system could be used in a variety of other ways.

Below: Major Ken Dudley, operating his unique remote control system, guides a Chieftain through the deep wading tank at the RAC Centre, Bovington Camp. / *Crown copyright*

Above: Loading a Chieftain on to the back of a tank transporter can be quite a tricky business as this photograph shows. / *Crown copyright*

Above right: Scammell's Contractor tank transporter. / *Scammell Motors*

Right: Once the tank is safely on board the securing chains must be fastened tightly. / *Crown copyright*

92

Left: A Centurion ARV begins to
pull a Chieftain out of trouble.
/ Simon Dunstan

93

Right: A Centurion ARV plus its crew of fitters change a Chieftain power pack at Suffield, Canada. / RTR Publications

Below: The Pilkington PE Ltd passive night driving periscope. This model is for the Chieftain ARV. It is the most successful of the new II night driving aids. / PE Pilkington Ltd

Passive Night Driving

Driving by night in the battle area has always been a difficult and dangerous business. Before the advent of infra-red driving aids the tank driver, unable to use his normal lights for obvious tactical reasons, could only peer into the gloom, taking his life (and those of the rest of the crew!) in his hands, as he negotiated difficult or unknown terrain. IR equipment certainly assisted the driver, but as it requires an active IR source, the chance of detection is now almost as great as if while light were used. Consequently, just as with the night viewing devices for the commander and gunner, there has been a lot of work done in producing passive, undectectable driving periscopes. The Pilkington PE Ltd passive night driving periscope is the latest and most successful of these new aids, and enables the tank driver to drive in the pitch dark, hatch down, without using any form of artificial illumination, and at speeds comparable with those achieved in daylight. As it does not emit any form of radiation it is completely undetectable. This periscope, now used in Chieftain, has a very fast objective lens which collects the small amount of light reflected from the night sky by the scene in front of the tank. This forms an image on the front end (photocathode) of the new single micro-channel image intensifier tube. Electrons, which are emitted by the photocathode, are then accelerated through a high voltage and form an image up to 60,000 times brighter, on the rear end (screen) of the tube. This image is then viewed through a magnifier which provides the necessary amount of magnification.

8. Communications

It has been said that communications are the lifeblood of an armoured formation. Certainly quick and reliable means of passing information and orders are essential on the battlefield, and in armoured units this means the widespread use of radio, because no other method can maintain such a high degree of flexibility. As all arms must be able to work and communicate together then the radio equipment throughout any army must be standardised. In the British Army the current family of radio sets is known as the Larkspur range. These sets were introduced in the 1950s and 1960s and are currently being replaced by the new Clansman range. In this short chapter I want to look at both the Larkspur and Clansman radios and their associated equipment as mounted in the Chieftain.

Basic Installation

A gun tank is normally equipped with two radios, one medium range and one short range, although the control harness (Type A) can accept three radio sets. This is so that the same harness can be used in both control and command tanks which are found in squadron and regimental headquarters, where a second medium range set is essential. The radios are connected by the harness to a central junction box and thence by cables inside the tank, to the crew control boxes. These are located close to the position which the particular crew member normally occupies in the tank. Attached to his box is his headgear and microphone assembly (or crewman's helmet). Additional equipment, also connected by the control harness, includes a tank telephone, which is mounted externally on the rear of the tank so that dismounted troops can contact the tank crew; a remote control facility with 600ft of cable; a rebroadcast unit which enables incoming messages on one set to be automatically rebroadcast out over the other radio. A

Larkspur Radios

The medium range set is the C42 No 2, which is a VHF, frequency modulated voice only radio. It has 481 separate channels, spaced every 50kHz. The older No 1 model had only half as many channels spaced every 100kHz. The frequency coverage is 36-60MHz. The set is simple to operate with visual tuning. It has a squelch circuit which gives silent listening until a signal is received, this greatly reduces operator fatigue during long radio watches. The set can be operated on high or low power transmission strengths, the latter cutting transmission range to about one quarter. There is a 'traffic/stand-by' switch to reduce the drain on the batteries when listening only is required (eg under radio silence), the set taking about 15sec to warm up again once the switch is put to 'traffic'. An automatic modulation control keeps the input from the microphones constant (thus there is no improvement if one shouts). In addition, an IC amplifier is incorporated giving intercommunication between all crew members. The normal antenna is an 8ft rod, mounted in an antenna base on top of the turret. There is also an elevated antenna for use with a 27ft telescopic mast. The radio is fitted with an antenna tuning device (ATU). The range, as for all VHF radios, will depend mainly upon siting, however, between two mobile vehicles a range of 10 to 15 miles (16-24km) is normal.

The short range set is the B47, a VHF, frequency modulated, transmitter-receiver, voice only radio. 181 channels are available at a 100kHz spacing throughout the frequency band of 38 – 56MHz. A crystal calibrator is incorporated to make accurate tuning very easy. As with the C42 it has simple visual tuning, a squelch circuit, high and low power transmission strengths, and automatic modulation control. The antenna is an 8ft rod, again mounted on top of the turret. The range between two vehicle-borne sets is about five miles (8km).

Before leaving the Larkspur range a few words on how the crew actually listen and speak over the various radios and IC. The commander has a special microphone with a built-in set selector switch. He can thus change from set to set or to IC, without having to alter the switch on the front of his control box inside the tank. The rest of the turret crew have simpler microphones and must use the switch on their respective control boxes to change sets. The driver can

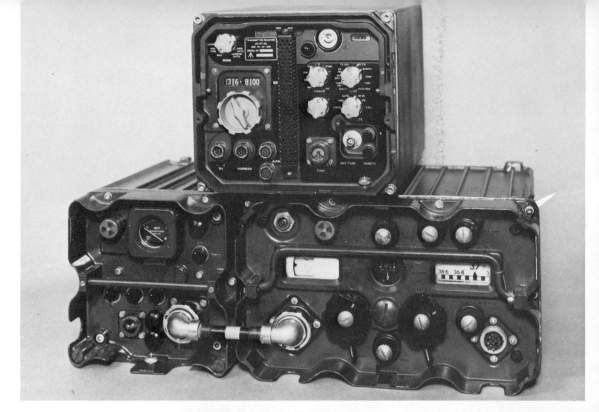

Above: A comparison photo showing clearly the relative sizes of the VRC353 and the C42 which it replaces. / *MSDS Stanmore*

Right: An operator changing frequency on the C42 radio inside a Chieftain. Note the charge bins by his feet. / *COI*

only speak on the IC. The commander has the further facility of being able to monitor all sets at once. All headsets and microphone assemblies have quick release plugs and snatch type harness, so that the crew can 'bale out' unimpeded in an emergency. These assemblies can also be fitted with a 30ft extension lead so that the crew can get off the tank and still remain able to work the radios.

Clansman

The introduction of the Larkspur range was a great step forward after the cumbersome, unreliable sets used by the Army during World War II. The introduction of the Clansman range is even more dramatic. A family of seven, smaller, lighter, more

Right: An operator changing frequency on the VRC353 in the turret of a Chieftain. The photo also provides a good view of the crewman's helmet and boom microphone. / *MSDS Stanmore*

Below: Using a tank telephone on the rear of Chieftain. Note: there is a 'call' button inside the box which the caller presses in order to attract the attention of the tank commander. The cable is about 10ft long, so that the caller can take cover in the nearest convenient ditch if under fire. However, the cable is spring loaded, so he must keep a tight grip on the rubberised telephone or it will be plucked from his grasp! / *Crown copyright*

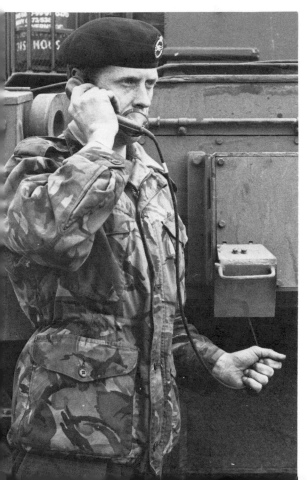

reliable and simpler to operate sets will replace the current family of 24 different models. A digital frequency synthesiser is at the heart of all Clansman sets, controlling the basic frequency extremely accurately. The synthesiser controls a variable-frequency oscillator which generates an output frequency. This is set accurately to a given frequency and then stabilised by means of a digital control-loop system, using a crystal-controlled oscillator as a reference standard. Design of the frequency oscillator varies according to the type of transmitter/receiver. Five sets are available in the VHF band, one being the UK/VRC 353 vehicle radio produced by Marconi Space and Defence Systems (the other four sets 349/350/351/352 are all manpacks). It is designed for use in all armoured or soft skinned vehicles. It operates over a frequency range of 30-76MHz, with 1,840 channels at a 25kHz spacing. It will however, operate at 50kHz channel spacing as well, thus ensuring interoperability with existing British and NATO equipments. The power output of 50W gives a range of at least 31 miles (50km) with the normal end-fed whip antenna, or more than 50 miles (80km) with an elevated antenna. A power switch enables other outputs of 15W, 1W and 0.1W to be selected, the last named being especially useful for 'whisper' communications between two vehicles. The sets are lightweight (22kg), extremely rugged, simple to operate and incorporate a fully automatic squelch. They have

97

automatic rebroadcast facilities and remote control, where the distance at which the set can be operated remotely is three miles (5km). Another feature of all vehicular sets is that they can be used together on the same vehicle with the minimum of mutual interference. This 'Electromagnetic Compatibility' (EMC) as it is called, is a major problem with multiple radio set installations. In the Clansman range, careful attention has been paid to EMC to suppress broadband noise, harmonics and other spurious effects from both transmitters and receivers. This has been achieved by careful design in both radio and antenna systems. Microminiaturisation has been used and special integrated circuits have been developed wherever necessary, to reduce the size, weight and power consumption of the sets. As will be seen by the comparison photograph between the C42 and VRC353, the set is at least one third smaller. The

VRC353 will replace both the C42 and B47 on Chieftain.

Environmental Specification

To get a true idea of how robust and rugged the new range really is, here are details of the environmental specifications which Clansman radios must meet and in some instances actually exceed! They must be capable of:

(a) operation and storage at an altitude of 2,500m
(b) immersion in water to a depth of 1.5m
(c) operation and storage over a temperature range of −40°C to +55°C (Ambient) plus the effects of Solar Radiation (1,130W/M² for six hours)
(d) transportation at an altitude of 7,250m
(e) tropical exposure — 84 days at 95% RH, temperature cycling from +20°C to +35°C
(f) operation and storage under conditions of heavy driving rain, salt spray, high wind, driving dust and driving snow
(g) meeting the corrosive effects of acid and alkaline spray and to be unaffected by severe contamination by fuel oils, hydraulic oils and lubricating oils
(h) meeting operational conditions in wheeled and tracked land vehicles travelling over surfaced and unsurfaced roads and open country, and transport by land, sea and air
(j) meeting operational shocks in AFVs due to the impact of non-penetrating shells on the vehicle armour and delivery by normal parachute techniques

Crewmen's Helmets

The British Army has only in recent years decided to go for protective helmets for their AFV crews. The initial helmet they chose was the 'Helmguard' originally made by Racal Amplivox for the Swedish Army, but modified with the addition of a boom microphone. The helmet provides both head and ear protection, the former being both from impact and penetration (must not be pierced by a 6mm ball at a velocity of 130m/sec). Ear protection is by means of the unique acoustic valve, which in the closed position provides ear protection against high ambient noise levels. When open, the user is able to hear important airborne noises such as speech warnings, commands etc, however, the ears are fully protected from unexpected loud noises, such as gunfire and explosions. With built-in earphones and the boom microphone, the helmet does away with the need to wear the normal microphone and headgear assembly. Inner detachable pads allow for size adjustment, whilst velcro-covered draw-straps make it easy to put on and take off. For hotter climes, a new ventilated tank helmet has been recently designed by Racal Amplivox and is now on trial in Iran. It could well eventually replace the Helmguard helmet.

Below: A close up of the ingenious microphone and adaptor to be used with a respirator, thus allowing all crew members to remain in communication without producing muffled speech.
/ *SG Brown Communications Ltd*

9. Latest Model

Below and overleaf: This excellent series of photographs shows all round views of the latest model of Chieftain, the Mark 5/2(K), at the Royal Ordnance Factory, Barnbow, Leeds, in August 1978. The tank is one of the batch ordered by Kuwait. Note the absence of the searchlight. / *Crown copyright*

10. The Crew

The crew of a Chieftain tank, like the crew of any other specialised vehicle must work as a team, if they are to get the best out of their vehicle and its equipment. For a tank crew this can make the difference between life and death.

The following accounts of the work of members of a tank crew are told by soldiers of my old regiment, the 4th Royal Tank Regiment — 'Scotland's Own Royal Tank Regiment' as is is popularly called. I was second in command of the regiment when we made the difficult change of role from armoured cars to tanks. After six years, serving all over the world, with exciting operational tours in Aden and Borneo, the regiment came down to earth with a bang, when faced with the task of becoming an armoured regiment again in the Rhine Army. After the relative simplicity of the Saladin armoured car and the Ferret scout car, learning about the Chieftain seemed a daunting proposition, with its heavier maintenance load and more complicated gunnery equipment. It was going to mean much more 'hard graft' for everyone, without the chance of being able to swan off at will, over the countryside. We had covered hundreds of miles in the beautiful Rhine and Moselle valleys on our final armoured car exercise before moving up to Hohne during a bleak and icy German winter. We took over from the 11th Hussars, 'those incomparable paladins' as Churchill had called them during their wartime days in armoured cars in the Western Desert. As we have already seen, they were the first regiment to be fully equipped with the new tank and had achieved a magnificent standard of competence and efficiency in their new role that we would find hard to emulate.

Now, some eight years later, the Fourth are one of the most experienced Chieftain regiments in the British Army and, dare I say it, one of the best. They have done very well and no doubt will continue to do so, in the down-to-earth, thoroughly professional way that so typifies the RTR approach to soldiering. Of course they grumble about the hard work, the long hours, the pay and all the rest, but they are still proud of their expertise and proud to be highly skilled, professional tankmen.

The photographs accompanying this chapter do not relate, I'm afraid, to the crew featured in the text. However, they do typify the life of a tank crew both on and off training, in and out of barracks.

Crew Duties — Main Tasks

The main tasks of a tank crew are:

Commander

Command the tank and crew. Receives and takes action on all orders. Map reads and guides the driver. Gives orders to the gunner and the loader. Keeps the troop leader fully informed of anything affecting his tank (eg: enemy action, state of fuel, ammunition, breakdowns, etc).

Driver

Drives the tank, choosing the best and quickest route to the objective or to the next firing position. Helps the commander by thinking ahead and driving sensibly. Carries out daily maintenance on the engine, transmission and running gear. Helps the fitters with any major repairs.

Gunner

Lays and fires the guns on orders from the commander. During some engagements makes his own corrections to hit targets and in others acts on orders from the commander. Carries out daily maintenance on guns, gunnery equipment and sighting gear.

Loader/Operator

Loads the main tank gun, the RMG and the coaxially mounted machine gun. Listens on the radio and answers for the commander if he is busy or away from the tank. Tunes the radios and keeps in good communication with other tanks in the troop, infantry, etc. Carries out daily maintenance on all radio equipment and helps the gunner with his maintenance. During firing he clears any stoppages occurring on the guns (less commander's MG).

Chieftain Tank Driver

Corporal Tony Smee has served all over the world with the Fourth, including tours in the Far East and Germany. Like most regular soldiers he is no stranger to Ulster and has recently completed his third tour there. After eight years' service he left the Army in late 1974, but rejoined in the spring of 1976. He writes:

'The first time I saw a Chieftain it was parked alongside my Guided Weapons Ferret. Somebody had the bright idea that we should familiarise ourselves before doing a full conversion course. So, when I came down the Vehicle Park and saw this monster I said to myself: "No way am I going near that!" But I was wrong.

'The driver training was hard, but when you look back it was a good course. Mine took place at Sennelager, West Germany, where there was plenty of scope for cross-country training but not much for road work. I started by learning the pedals and how to use the instruments on the dashboard. After the cramped seat of the Ferret it was like sitting in a bloody great plush armchair. I'm told that the design of the seat was taken from a dentist's chair, it certainly has just as many different positions. Without a clutch pedal my gear changing was a bit jerky at first, but I soon got the hang of it. The gear selector pedal is on the left-hand side; to change up you press it up with your foot and vice-versa to change down. All this is done in

conjunction with the engine revs, as laid down in the instructional manuals, which tell you to watch your tachometer and only to change gear at so and so revs. Personally, I find it better to listen to the engine note, rather than just use the tacho on its own.

'During the course most driving was done with the gun to the rear, safely locked in the gun crutch, rather than to the front on stabiliser. This was because some of the trainee drivers, who couldn't judge the movement of the gun on stab, kept digging the end of the barrel into the ground and collecting half a ton of shit up it. This was guaranteed not to please the instructor! Driving with the hatch open was quite easy once you had mastered the art of driving by ear, concentrating on the engine note and trying not to be put off by the radio "chat" coming over your headsets. Also one got the feel of the steering tillers, and if they needed bleeding you could compensate by pumping them continuously as you motored along. Once your instructor thought you were good enough he let you drive with the gun in front and this is when it really became hard, as the gun sticks out such a heck of a long way — about three metres over the end of the hull — so you really have to watch it.

'A gunnery instructor will say that the tank driver is there to maintain a stable platform for the turret crew. To my mind that can be one of the hardest jobs

imaginable, when you are moving fast across country and making full tactical use of the ground. A driver knows that if he changes gear with a jerk just as the gunner has pressed the tit, when the target will be missed and that could prove fatal. To drive smoothly at speed, across rough country, so that the gunnery boffins can track their moving targets and all the rest of it requires a bionic brain!

'Closed down driving was made worse by the fact that they took away our bonnets and gave us these Dan Dare helmets. The first problem before closing down is repositioning the steering tillers to the closed down position. This normally requires some expert attention with a sledge hammer, 7lb. The tillers are now much further back and, even with the seat right down, they never seem to bear much relation to the length of one's arms. The seat itself is lowered to the floor and the headrest supports the helmet. Then the hatch has to be shut — on most tanks this requires bullworker lessons! Everything is now completely different. The view through the periscope is quite limited and it needs experience to get used to it. The noise of the engine revs is much quieter, but you can still drive by ear if you listen carefully. For some unknown reason the pedals always seem harder to find and some learner drivers get a mild state of claustrophobia, small wonder really, with the hatch closed over your head, the ammo bins crowding in on both sides and the smell of the batteries, which, in my opinion have a poor ventilation system.

'The driver is now virtually lying flat on his back, looking at an angle through his periscope, so he doesn't see the ground immediately in front of the tank, but is looking some 20 metres ahead all the time. You have to try to remember what you have seen, because you won't hit that particular bit of ground for another few seconds. It also makes the shape of the ground much harder to read and a ridge the size of a plough furrow tends to become larger in the mind — so you approach it carefully, changing down and creeping along — only to find that the tank takes it with no bother at all and you get a blast from the commander to stop hanging about and speed up. That make you feel a right 'nana, so the next time the ridge really is as steep as it looks but you think "to hell with it", speed up and wallop! — much bad language from the rest of the crew — honestly, you just can't win.

'You also have the problem of not knowing the direction the gun is pointing, so you have to use your gun position indicator, which takes a bit of remembering at first. You will be driving along all going well, when you feel a little thump, hear a noise of grating gears and realise that you have forgotten to look and the gun is pirouetting about — more curses from upstairs.

'The dashboard now stares brilliantly at you — all the illuminated dials, gauges and instruments seem to grow in size. I know that trainee drivers get a bit scared of it all in case it's one big balls up, which at the start is usually the case. The speed of the tank in low gear gives you the impression that you are not moving at all, whilst in high gear that you are about to sprout wings and become Stingray. You make more of a jerk when gear changing too, because you can't hear the engine note quite so clearly until you become experienced. You rev up like mad, can't hear anything, look at the tacho, say "Jesus Christ", slam up the gear change pedal and end up with your eyeballs on the sight, looking cross-eyed at your nose, with a large bump on the head, plus, of course, lots more abuse from the turret, but it all comes with practice. When operating closed down you are normally in contact or expecting contact at any moment. I have personally been closed down for 48 hours at a stretch on an exercise. It takes a bit of getting used to in many ways, and you really must keep an eye on your instruments. If good maintenance parades have been done and nothing serious goes wrong, then there is no problem to driving for long periods closed down, but like everything else it takes experience to know what to look for. One of the biggest problems is not knowing the state of your tracks and how tight you can turn with a slack track, or what angle to approach an obstacle. Once a track goes, it can take a long time to get back on the road again.

'Night driving is different again, you've either got it or you haven't. With the aids we have nowadays you can see OK, but it's a matter of getting as much practice as possible. The night driving periscope doesn't show the dips and bumps as such. You have to be able to read the shadows on a weird green landscape and even experienced drivers can make a mistake and get bogged. The eyes become very tired after a couple of hours and your concentration drops off. Even when driving open up at night, just following the convoy light of the tank in front tends to hypnotise you. You follow and follow and don't realise that he has stopped, until your gun muzzle is right up his arse and you have spilt the new brew of coffee which was in the gun cradle. The way to drive at night is basically to feel you way carefully into every dip and to come out with bags of confidence. I prefer to let the engine labour a bit in 3rd or 4th gears, hardly ever using 1st or 2nd at night. It may not be in the rule-book, but it is normally only for a very limited period and it makes the tank that much easier to control.

'First and last parades are always done exactly as per the servicing schedule, whether in barracks or out on training, so that everything that has to be done gets done at the right time. As one gains experience you get to know what to look for, finding the fault before it can develop into a major repair job. On a large exercise when you are going non-stop, then there is no time for formal first and last parades, so the driver must use every opportunity to get out, lift the engine and transmission decks and look for faults. He must also keep a continuous watch on the tracks, especially on track pins and circlips during a long road march. Continuous checking is the secret and knowing how long you can keep going with a leak of some kind, before calling the fitters in. Naturally you always try to keep going to the next leaguer, when there will hopefully be time to have a proper look at the fault and to get it repaired.

'A good driver is worth his weight in gold, particularly if he can cope without a lot of prompting from his commander.'

Chieftain Loader — A Battle Run

'The time is 0500hrs and it is just getting light as the guard goes round the individual tank positions waking up the crews. The place is our squadron bivouac area on the NATO Tank Gunnery Ranges at Hohne in North Rhine Westphalia. For us tank crews it is an important day, the last of our annual open range firing period, and it includes the hardest test of all — a fully tactical battle run.

'Crews are soon out of their tank shelters washing, shaving and preparing breakfast. The tank

Left: Loaded! A Blues and Royals
loader loads an APDS projectile.
/ *COI*

Below: Loader/operator adjusting
the controls of his C42 radio. / *COI*

commanders collect together their maps, notebooks, chinagraph pencils and all the rest of the clobber they will need for the troop leader's Orders group. He has already told us that he will brief the complete troop on his return from attending the squadron leader's "O" group.

'Everyone is busy on first parade, checking the tanks and preparing the guns for firing, when he returns and calls us all together. It is then we find that we are to be the first troop down the Battle Run, so we shall be setting the standard for the rest of the squadron.

'By 0730hrs all preparations have been made, our three tanks are fully stowed, crews mounted and ready for the off. Over the IC our commander reminds us of what we can expect to see on the range. The targets will mainly be "pop-ups" — hessian screens in the shape of enemy tanks that will appear as we get in range — some of them will be "puffed", using gunfire simulators to make them more realistic. When we hit these targets a strike indicator will automatically trigger off a small cloud of coloured smoke as an indication of a good hit. A few of the targets are old tank hulks, but as these are very expensive to maintain and take a hell of a pounding, they are normally kept on the static target ranges and used for initial AP engagements, as it is essential for both gunners and commanders to know exactly what a strike on real armour plate looks like.

'It has started to rain heavily and the sight heaters have to be switched on to prevent the sights from misting up. There is a certain amount of tenseness among the crew, as we wait impatiently for the order to get going. Inevitably small things start to go wrong — our commander curses a leaking episcope seal in his cupola that has let the rain in, dripping all over his carefully marked map. The gunner reports that the laser sight is giving false readouts, no doubt caused by the rain. This is more serious, but no sweat really, as we can always use our standby method of ranging — the trusty .50 Ranging Machine Gun, which I have mounted, well oiled and ready to fire, alongside the main gun. I'm the loader/operator by the way, which means that in addition to looking after the tank radios I have to load and clear stoppages on the main 120mm gun, the RMG and the coaxially mounted GPMG — quite a hairy job when the action really hots up.

' "24 ALPHA move off now", comes the order over the radio and away we go. The driver's initial gear changes are a bit jumpy as the gearbox oil is still cold and the electrics haven't warmed up yet. He must try to give us the smoothest ride possible, as a bad gear change can make all the difference between a hit or a miss and the commander will have his guts for garters if he doesn't get it right! Just before we move off the commander opens his cupola lid and reaches out to

Above left: Bazooka plates prepared for the addition of foliage as sideplate camouflage. / *Capt J. C. W. Gillman*

Left: The back decks of Chieftain, plus a tarpaulin slung over the gun makes a dry, warm but inelegant 'tent' for a quick kip during exercises. / *Capt J. C. W. Gillman*

Above: A typical tank bivouac can be seen at the side of this Chieftain. / *Capt J. C. W. Gillman*

Right: The best part of a bazooka plate is that it makes a very handy table to keep all the cooking gear off the damp ground! / *Capt J. C. W. Gillman*

change the range safety flag on the turret from green to red, indicating that we are now "at action", just a small part of the rigorously enforced range safety procedure so important on all tank gunnery ranges.

'Off we go, crossing the start line on time, all the crew keyed up and waiting for the first engagement. I get the order to half load the machine guns so that keeps me busy. Suddenly the turret swings around to the right, as the commander uses his overrider to lay the gun on to a target he has spotted. "RANGING SABOT TANK ON!" he shouts, and the crew spring into action. The driver, using his initiative, gets into a reasonable hull down position close by — no sense in hanging about in the open waiting to be shot at. The gunner is busy acquiring the target in his sights and laying on accurately. I have so much to do it isn't true. First the RMG, which I had half-loaded on the start line must be fully loaded; then I must select APDS Practice projectile from the rack and ram it into the open breech, followed by the correct bag charge; close the breech, make the trip by pulling across the loader's safety shield and flick off the loader's safety switch — the gun won't fire until that has been done — and finally shout "LOADED!" All that takes just a few seconds and I'm now standing by the gun, another APDS proj in my arms, waiting for the next order.

' "ON, FIRING NOW!" shouts the gunner and begins firing the laid down sequence of three, three-round bursts with the RMG, fired at ever increasing ranges, in order to determine the exact target range. He gets a strike at "DOT 2", switches the weapon selector switch across to "Main" and fires. The quiet thump, thump, thump of the RMG is replaced by the sharp, heavy crack of the main gun, and a SABOT screams away to the target. The gun recoils and the breech open automatically, I slam home another DS proj, plus its bag charge, make the trip etc, and again shout "LOADED!" "STOP!" shouts the commander, after the second round has been fired, "Well done everyone, that was a first round hit in under six seconds — a bloody good start!" We are highly chuffed with our success.

'The stink of cordite fills the turret, but it's not as bad as it used to be, thanks to the very efficient fume extractor and the turret fans which are going full blast. No empty cases to ditch either, thank goodness — that's another good feature of Chieftain. Off we go again, moving into another fire position to engage some figure targets immediately to our front with the coax. The commander lets us get on with this shoot by ourselves as he is busy spotting for the troop leader who is engaging a target off to our left front.

' "24 ALPHA, move to the next bound", comes the order from our troop leader. The driver reverses out of the fire position, down behind the crest and works his way round the side of the hill, we always do this when leaving a position as it makes it more difficult for an enemy observer to spot us. As we motor along I check the guns over, give them a squirt of oil for luck, refill the ready round bins, maker certain that there aren't any empty cartridge cases blocking the passageways to the spent cartridge bags, or that the belts aren't fouling anywhere or twisted — no sense in getting a stoppage for a bloody silly reason like that. We halt in a turret down position and the commander carefully scans the countryside through his periscope. Whilst this is happening we hear on the radio that our BRAVO tank has had a misfire. I can imagine how the crew feel, wondering if they have carried out the drills correctly, or if the bag charge is damp, or if the firing circuit is defective, or any of the other possible reasons for the failure. A couple of minutes later we hear that it was a faulty vent tube loader and they are given permission to load it by hand.

'The other crew's difficulties are quickly forgotten, as our commander spots another target and we move up to hull down to engage it. The target this time is a pair of anti-tank guns, some distance away and outside the range of our RMG. It will be a HESH target and because of the range we shall have to bracket it with HESH and then fire three rounds "fire for effect". This calls for some pretty snappy loading on my part. We open up and watch the tracer curving through the sky towards the target.

' "STOP! Both targets destroyed, well done lads", orders the commander at the end of the shoot after the three-round salvo has landed smack on top of the screens, blowing them high in the air.

'More fire and movement follows as we go down the run, until we approach the final bound which involves another long-range shoot. As it is our last engagement we are given permission to expend all our ammunition. I can barely see for the sweat and have several bleeding knuckles after that lot, but I don't notice them until much later on, as the job calls for total concentration.

'Once the run is completed we clear guns and move back down to the start line for a debrief with the IG (Instructor Gunnery) who has been following behind us in a Ferret scout car, watching our firing and making sure that we were following all the range safety rules. From there it is back to the bivouac area for gun cleaning, comparing notes with the other crews and a can of the commander's Tennents Lager — a perfect end to a very satisfying and useful day.'

Chieftain Gunner

Trooper Ted Reid joined the Fourth in 1972 and has served in Berlin and all over West Germany with the Regiment. His tank soldiering has been interspersed with tours in Northern Ireland and he has recently returned from his third operational tour there. He writes:

'My experience as a gunner started in Berlin when I was nominated for a B3 course. At first I wasn't keen to do it, because I didn't much fancy the idea of being stuck in the gunner's seat all the time, as it is so confined. The first few weeks of the course were mainly classroom work, sitting on your bottom — like being back at school really. But after we got on to the CIMs* it was well worth it. The CIM periods were

* CIM — Classroom Instructional Mounting (see Chapter 13)

good fun, putting all the theory we had learned into practice. I really enjoyed firing with the .22 bracket, the little rubber targets wobbled from side to side when you hit them — great!

'Most of the basic gunnery course was spent in learning the loading and unloading drills on the 120mm, the RMG and GPMG. No matter how good you thought you were at the drills there was always room for improvement. We had to learn the stripping and assembling of the weapons and the six- and eight-point safety checks. We also spent a few periods learning to recognise the different AFVs of the main

Left: The caption for this photo read 'a gunner of a Chieftain tank about to engage a hard target'. It is an excellent shot of the gunner and his controls, but unfortunately he has no sight fitted, so he would be rather pushed to engage anything! / COI

Below: A good photo of a 5RIDG commander and gunner in their respective seats in the turret of their Chieftain. / COI

countries in the world. Some were very hard to distinguish, particularly when they were properly camouflaged. We used small cardboard backed pictures of them which were set out on a FMR (Field Miniature Range) made up to look like real countryside.

'After all the theory and indoor work we went on the open range for our first live firing period. I was fourth in line to fire and the bangs of the Chieftain guns were very noisy from outside the tank, so I was getting a bit worried that they would be even louder inside. Everyone who had fired told me that there was nothing to worry about, but I wasn't going to believe them until I had done it myself. At last it was my turn, so I climbed on board and jumped down into the gunner's seat. I got the order for action, laid my sights on the first target and began going through the procedure I had learned on the course. It really calmed me down and got everything together, so that when I got the order to fire I was quite calm. I did my final lay, shouted "FIRING NOW!" and pressed the tit. To my amazement there was hardly any noise at all inside the tank and not as much recoil as I had expected. The AP practice round flies so fast that you really have to watch carefully to see where it strikes if you miss the target. My first round kicked up a small spurt of dust just to the left of the old tank hulk we were engaging. "RIGHT ONE!" I shouted, so that the commander would know that I had seen where the first round had landed and was making a correction of one target's width to the right. "STOP! RIGHT HALF TARGET GO ON!" he shouted back, I had overcorrected and might have wasted another round had he not stepped in. I repeated his correction, adjusted my sights and fired again. The next second the turret of the old hulk erupted in a blinding orange flash, a sure sign, even with DS practice, that the round had hit the target.

' "Well done gunner, a good hit," said the instructor, "now let's try something a bit more difficult." He took me through a series of engagements against static and moving targets, using DS practice, HESH and GPMG. I used my laser sight throughout — what a fantastic piece of kit it is, a spot-on range readout in a split second, no problem. I was surprised how tired I felt when my practices were finished and it was time to let the next man take my place. I had really enjoyed my first session in the gunner's seat. Now I wouldn't swop places with anyone — after all it's what a tank is all about isn't it? Without a good gunner the rest might as well go home, and with Simfire* fitted I can go through all my open range practices on exercises as well.

* See Chapter 13 for a description of Simfire and its successor Simfics.

'After I had finished my gunnery course I was put on the troop corporal's tank as his gunner. I was looking forward to our first Hohne firing period, as my squadron had been nominated, along with two squadrons from other regiments, to compete for selection to represent the British Army in the Canadian Army Trophy — a tank gunnery competition which is held every year and competed for by tank squadrons from six of the NATO nations. We were up early on our first morning at Hohne, checking the tanks over carefully to be sure that all was OK to fire. We were going on to a battle run, with three tanks in each troop all doing the run together. We were on the right and our targets were a mixture of head-on movers, side-on movers, static hulks and various machine gun targets. We soon reached the first bound, the first target was puffed and my commander gave me the order "RANGING SABOT TANK ON!" I replied "ON!" as soon as I had put the MBS (Muzzle Bore Sight) mark on the target and waited for the loader to report "LOADED!" Then I pressed the "Lase" button on my TLS (Tank Laser Sight) in order to get the range to the target. This took a couple of seconds or so and I then shouted it out to the commander, who checked it back to me — he does this to ensure that I haven't made a balls up — then I did my final lay and fired. With APDS it is really quite difficult to miss! After a few engagements we moved on and were attacked by enemy infantry en route to the next bound. I fired at them with my coax, but it is not easy to hit such small targets on the move. Battle runs certainly improve your gunnery and our engagement times were soon down to a few seconds. We also had to do a night shoot, with carefully worked out arcs of fire. It wasn't easy to see the targets in the darkness until the artillery fired some illuminating shells and we could then open up on them. It is great firing at night, you can watch the trace as the rounds go down range and when you get a strike the sparks fly all over the place!

'The highspot of our training was undoubtedly going to the Suffield Training Area in Canada. It was the first time I had fired Service APDS as it's a bit too powerful for the ranges in Germany. The Suffield exercises were so realistic that you actually felt as though you were in a real battle. We were closed down most of the time, with the other tanks firing all round us. With infantry, engineers, artillery and all the rest of the battlegroup taking part in the exercises and all firing live ammo, it must be as near the real thing as it is possible to get. The night battles were fantastic too and had to be seen to be believed. We fired into a killing zone and some of the tank hulks had been primed with petrol so that they burst into flames when you hit them.'

11. People and Parades

Below: Her Majesty The Queen inspects her Chieftains. Accompanied by The Duke of Edinburgh and Gen Sir Roland Gibbs, Her Majesty takes a close look at part of her armoured forces during the Silver Jubilee Review of the Army at Sennelager, July 1977. / *Crown copyright*

Above: On parade in Berlin. A troop of Chieftains belonging to A Squadron 4RTR, photographed in front of the Brandenberg Gate, 1974. / *Crown copyright*

Right: Line up of 17/21 Lancers' Chieftains at Sennelager, June 1968. / *COI*

Below right: James McCowan of Dewar's Whisky has a taste of something a little weaker during his visit to 4RTR. / *4RTR*

12. Variants

ARMOURED VEHICLE LAUNCHED BRIDGE (AVLB)

Crew: 3
Weapons: One 7.62mm GPMG; multi-barrelled smoke dischargers
Weight: 53,300kg (52.25 tons) (with No 8 bridge)
Length: 13.74m (45.34ft) (with No 8 bridge)
Height: 3.885m (12.82ft) (with No 8 bridge)

	No 8 Bridge	No 9 Bridge
Length of Max Span		
(with good bank seats)	22.9m (75ft)	12.2m (40ft)
Width of Bridge (both)	4.16m (13.73ft)	
Width of Roadway		
(both)	4m (13.2ft)	
Weight	12,200kg	9,144kg
	(11.96 tons)	(8.96 tons)

The Chieftain Bridgelayer (FV4205) is based upon a normal Chieftain Mark 5 tank without its turret and has a comparable performance with the gun tank. ROF Leeds built the prototype and have subsequently been responsible for all production, the first models being delivered in 1974. Lockheed Precision Products and Tubes (Birmingham) Hydraulic Controls Department, were also involved in the development. The hydraulically operated bridge launching and recovery mechanism is fitted to the glacis plate and secured to the hull. The main hydraulic pump is driven through a step-up gearbox by a power takeoff from the main engine. Two secondary pumps, one electrically driven and the other manually operated, are fitted as alternate power supplies. The AVLB can be fitted with two types of tank bridge, the No 8 Scissors bridge and the No 9 Boom Launch bridge. Both are Class 80 bridges and can be used by all A and B vehicles. The AVLB takes about 3-5min to lay a bridge across a gap and about 10min to recover it. Recovery can be from either end. Having laid one bridge, the AVLB is then available to be loaded with another and this flexibility is highlighted by the fact that it is normally deployed as part of a 'bridge train', comprising the AVLB, one No 8 bridge, two No 9 bridges, a tractor and trailer to carry the spare bridges (see photos). Both bridges are made of an aluminium-zinc-magnesium alloy and maraging steel.

Below: AVLB with a No 8 Scissors bridge in the travelling position. The bridge will span a 22.9m (75ft) gap. / *Crown copyright*

Above: A No 8 bridge being carried by the tractor and trailer which forms an essential part of an AVLB 'bridge train'. / *Crown copyright*

Left: An AVLB with a No 9 Boom Launch bridge in the travelling position. The bridge will span a 12.2m (40ft) gap. / *Crown copyright*

Above right: Launching a No 8 bridge during a demonstration at Bovington. / *Soldier*

Right: As the AVLB settles over the gap a Chieftain, just visible behind the bridgelayer, makes ready to cross. / *Simon Dunstan*

Right: Chieftain ARV.
/ *Simon Dunstan*

ARMOURED RECOVERY VEHICLE (ARV)
Crew: 4
Weapons: One cupola mounted 7.62mm GPMG, multi-barrelled smoke dischargers
Weight: 50,250kg (49.26 tons) empty
52,000kg (50.98 tons) loaded
Length: 8.256m (27.24ft)
Width: 3.518m (11.61ft)
Height: 2.746m (9.06ft)
Speed: 41.5kph (29.94mph)
Range: 320km (200 miles) (on roads)
160km (100 miles) (cross country)

The Armoured Recovery Vehicle, Chieftain, Mark 5 (FV4204) enables recovery operations to be carried out in the battle area and is provided for use by armoured regiments and armoured engineer squadrons. The first prototype was completed in 1971 and the ARV has been in production since 1974. The ARV is based on the normal gun tank, with the powerpack, L60 engine, fuel system, cooling system, hydraulic system-automotive, H30 engine (generating unit), transmission, suspension and driver's controls-automotive, identical to those fitted to the Mark 5 tank. The ARV is fitted with a 30-ton main capstan winch and a three-ton auxiliary capstan winch. The winches are forward operating and are located in a compartment at the front right hand side of the vehicle. The main winch is mechanically driven, via a power take-off and a propeller shaft, by the main

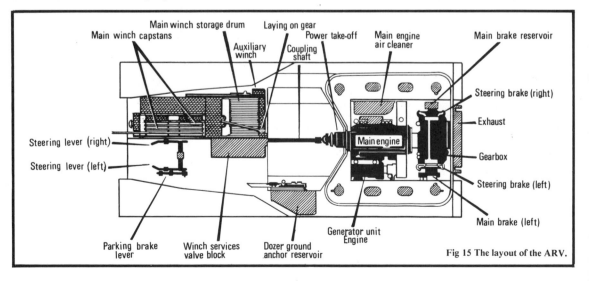

Fig 15 The layout of the ARV.

engine. Coupled to the drive are hydraulic pumps which supply power to operate the auxiliary winch. A detachable roof plate allows removal of the winch assemblies. The vehicle is also fitted with a dozer/ground anchor blade which is hydraulically operated. The crew compartment is at the rear of the driver's compartment and extends the full width of the hull. The commander is provided with a cupola, fitted in the roof plate, which allows all-round observation while under cover.

THE DOZER BLADE

Any Chieftain gun tank can be fitted with a dozer blade attachment designed by Automotive Products Ltd, which fits on to the front of the hull. Fitting takes about six hours. The kit comprises: an electro-hydraulic powerpack (fitted in place of the right hand front stowage bins); an aluminium blade with a steel cutting edge; a joystick control unit, operated by the driver. The dozer attachment can then be used for a variety of minor earth moving tasks, such as the dozing of tank scrapes for use as fire positions, rapid clearance of blocked lines of communication, filling-in minor defiles such as small streams and anti-tank ditches, the preparation and improvement of river crossing points.

Below: A Chieftain dozer, with its blade folded in the travelling position, kicks up the dust as it speeds along. / *COI*

Bottom: View of the Chieftain dozer blade. / *Simon Dunstan*

THE SHIR*

To date information has been released about two marks of this derivative of Chieftain. The Shir (Lion), of course will only be in service with the Iranian Army. Details are:

Mark 1

This is the combat improved Chieftain (FV4030), which incorporates the following new features I have already explained in preceding chapters — IFCS (the fully integrated fire control system made by Marconi Space Defence Systems Ltd); the Rolls-Royce 1,200bhp CV12 engine; the David Brown TN37 automatic gearbox and, it is hoped, the new Dunlop hydro-pneumatic suspension. The tank has conventional armour, giving it an all up weight of about 55 tons. The cooling group for the Shir was designed by Airscrew Howden and is a three belt driven mixed flow fan system of unique design. It

Above: The FV4030 which was originally developed for the Iranian Army.

allows for deep, compact radiators to be used and readily accommodates the pressure resistance of effective ballistic protection, without sacrificing cooling capacity. The total system is 'optimised' by using Airscrew computer assisted technology to minimise fan power and thus maximise power at the tracks.

Mark 2

As above, plus Chobham armour, thus increasing the weight to over 60 tons. The Mark 1 should be in full production by 1979 and the Mark 2 in 1980.

* The comments made in the footnote to Chapter 4 apply equally here.

118

13. Training Aids

The high cost and complexity of modern tanks, the increasing power of their weapon systems, the damage they do to roads and to the countryside, the dwindling number of suitable training areas where they can be properly exercised, all these factors present serious obstacles to the efficient training of tank crews in peacetime. One way of overcoming at least some of these problems is by the increased use of training simulators. In this chapter I would like to examine briefly three types of simulation equipment in current use, all of which have made a major contribution to the successful training of Chieftain crews. They are: the Link-Miles Driving Simulator; Classroom Instructional Mountings designed and produced by Wharton Engineers (Elstree) Ltd and by Morfax Ltd of Mitcham; and, lastly, the Simfire and Simfics Tactical and Gunnery trainers made by the Solartron Electronic Group Ltd of Farnborough.

The Link-Miles Driving Simulator

With a highly successful background in flight simulation, Link-Miles has been active in the driving simulation field since 1965, when they produced their first simulators based on the Chieftain, with analogue computation. Since then techniques have been greatly improved by the introduction of the digital computer and by the successful application of the advanced flight simulation expertise of their parent company — The Singer Company (UK) Ltd — to land based vehicles. The driving simulator can be used for initial driver training, conversion and continuation training, giving drivers practice over widely differing types of terrain, weather and driving conditions, and can be used 24 hours a day, seven days a week if necessary.

Below: The Link Miles Driving Simulator. A general view of the terrain model, showing the head of the TV camera on its gantry.
/ *Crown copyright*

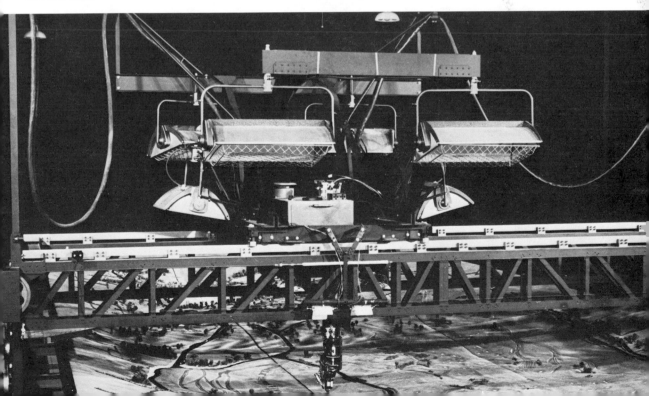

Far right: Fig 16 Digital tank simulator.

Right: Driver's module of the driving simulator. Note the driver's hatch and front glacis slope are identical to the real tank (so is the inside). / *Crown copyright*

Below: The Link Miles Driving Simulator. Instructor's console, note the TV screen, map of terrain model, Chieftain instrument panel (below screen). The two banks of knobs and switches enable the instructor to monitor progress, introduce faults etc. Note also the microphones and loudspeaker for two way communication with the trainee driver. / *Crown copyright*

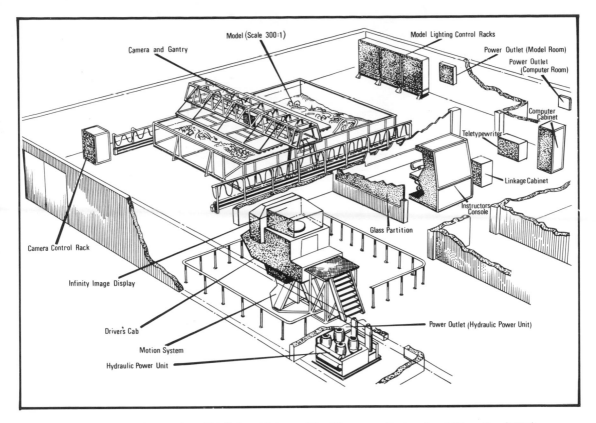

Camera and Gantry
Model (Scale 300:1)
Model Lighting Control Racks
Power Outlet (Model Room)
Power Outlet (Computer Room)
Computer Cabinet
Teletypewriter
Linkage Cabinet
Instructors Console
Glass Partition
Camera Control Rack
Infinity Image Display
Driver's Cab
Motion System
Hydraulic Power Unit
Power Outlet (Hydraulic Power Unit)

As the photographs show, the Chieftain driving simulator consists of five basic elements: a driving compartment fitted out with all the controls, instruments and equipment found in the tank; a terrain model representing a suitable stretch of varied countryside; an instructor's console, incorporating not only the means of monitoring the student's progress, but also of introducing faults and other hazards in order to test his reactions; a closed-circuit television link-up, so that both student and instructor are presented with a realistic view of the terrain model; and, finally, the computer. The layout of these components can be seen in Fig 16. The TV camera is fitted to a gantry above the terrain model and is then driven around the model at ground level by the trainee using his normal vehicle controls. It is possible to introduce noise, pitch and roll to the driving module in order to heighten the realism. The simulator thus allows the student to get many miles of safe, practical driving experience under his belt, and to become fully used to the controls and instruments, without ever once taking a tank out of a hangar, thus saving many expensive track miles. A rough indication of this saving is that one hour's training on the simulator is equivalent to six miles' training on the actual tank.

The Classroom Instructional Mounting (CIM)

The Chieftain CIM is intended to provide a relatively inexpensive means of training turret crews in their basic drills, shooting techniques and safety procedures. It consists of a simulated turret of exact size, shape and contour as the real thing, mounted on a stand which gives true height off the ground. The turret mounts a 120mm gun with standard breech mechanism, but a shortened, modified barrel, plus drill purpose .50in RMG and 7.62mm coaxial GPMG. Cut-out portions in the turret armour allow the instructor to supervise the crew under taining from his control console which is mounted on the rear of the turret. He can control the recoil and runout of the gun, simulate faults in the firing circuit and override all turret functions. The turret is fitted out to represent accurately the interior of the actual Chieftain tank, and both it and the commander's cupola have the same degree of rotational freedom as their real counterparts. The gun elevates and depresses as on the real tank, and loading, aiming, firing mechanisms, etc, are all faithfully reproduced. Recoil of the gun on firing is accurately simulated by a hydraulic system, and the charges/rounds are recycled from the end of the cut down barrel. The simulated bag charges and

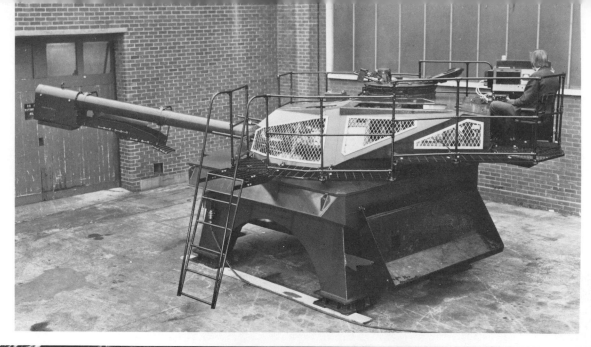

Left: Classroom Instructional Mounting. An excellent view of the Gunnery CIM, note the instructor's console, the cut-out portions in the turret armour (so that the rest of the class can see inside) and the modified barrel with ammunition shute. / *Morfax Ltd*

Below left: The slow recoil facility being demonstrated on the Chieftain Gunnery CIM. This allows students to examine the action of the recoil mechanism in slow time.
/ *Wharton Engineers (Elstree) Ltd*

Right: Armament CIM made by Wharton's is used by the REME to instruct gunfitters and armament artificers.
/ *Wharton Engineers (Elstree) Ltd*

Below: Instrument CIM made by Wharton's and used by the REME to train Instrument Mechanics.
/ *Wharton Engineers (Elstree) Ltd*

projectiles accurately represent the range of ammunition carried by the tank in weight, colour and shape.

The CIM is fitted with a special bracket incorporating a standard 7.62mm SLR (Self Loading Rifle) fitted with a Heckler-Koch conversion kit to allow .22in ammunition to be fired at targets on a miniature range. (This bracket can also be fitted to a real tank for miniature range shooting). A relatively new innovation is a pulse generator, which allows the instructor to inject artificially into the gunner's sight the range readout from the laser sight, because it is impossible to flash the real laser inside a building, so artificial means must be used. In addition, the CIM can be mounted on a rocking base to simulate the effects of vehicle motion. Thus, the whole turret crew can be practised in their tasks in very realistic conditions.

As well as the basic CIM for the training of tank crews, Wharton's make both an armament CIM and an instrument CIM for the training of REME gunfitters, armament artificers and instrument mechanics on the Chieftain tank. The CIM is a vital link in the training 'chain' and provides regiments of the Field Force, as well as more static training establishments, with an invaluable continuation trainer on which the vast majority of current gunnery techniques can be practised. Each regiment has two CIMs and they are in constant use.

For the future, work is in progress to find a replacement for the .22in rifle bracket and miniature range, in view of escalating costs, safety and the need to get away from expensive buildings. It is possible that some form of low intensity gas laser will be used to produce a light spot on to a cinema screen, a system which will allow far more flexibility. Another new development is in the field of computer generated imagery (CGI).

The Simfire and Simfics trainers

The Solartron Simfire and its successor Simfics have three main roles viz: first and foremost as a tactical trainer which simulates the casualty producing effects of live ammunition on training exercises, thus forcing all those taking part to react realistically as though they really were under the threat of live attack;

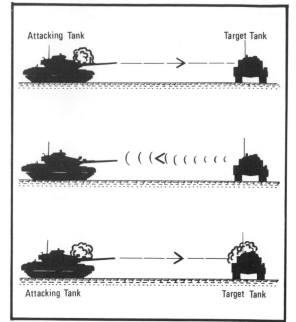

Above: Fig 17 How Simfire works.

Left: Simfire. A close up of a Chieftain turret, showing the Weapon Projector in its mounting and guard, mounted on the barrel of the 120mm; two of the five detector units can be seen on either side of the turret; just below the commander is the Radio receiver/transmitter unit complete with antenna and guard; finally the Flash Generator (on the right of the photo) filled with flash cartridges. / Solartron Electronic Group

Above right: Simfire. Bale out! With the smoke pyrotechnic belching coloured smoke (for 30 seconds) simulating a kill, the crew of this Chieftain bale out. / Solartron Electronic Group

Right: Simfics. A Chieftain, equipped with the latest Simfics equipment. The most obvious difference to Simfire equipment is that the weapon projector is fitted inside the barrel of the 120mm rather than on top. / Solartron Electronic Group

secondly, it greatly increases the realism and sense of purpose of all armoured training, generating a high level of motivation on the part of those under training as well as enabling those in charge to assess the standards achieved; finally, as a gunnery trainer it allows frequent and realistic practising of all standard gunnery procedures against real targets without the need to commit large areas of land for firing ranges, or without the expense of live ammunition. The current equipment, the Simfire Mk 11 ER (Extended Range), is the third generation of Simfire and incorporates many improvements over earlier models; the range has been increased to 2,400m and ballistic simulation and fall of shot indication are greatly improved.

The sequence of events in a typical Simfire engagement is as follows:

1 Tank Commander sees the target
2 He gives the fire order in the normal way
3 On the Simfire Control Unit, the loader sets in the range and presses the load button to select the required type of ammunition
4 After a preset delay of a few seconds (to simulate the time taken to load a round of ammunition), the 'loaded' light on the Control Unit will come on, indicating that the gun is ready to be fired. One round is deducted from the quantity of ammunition available

5 In the Projector a cam is set to deflect the laser through an angle that compensates for the elevation of the gun
6 The Gunner lays on to the target
7 The Gunner presses the firing switch
8 The Projector emits a series of laser pulses, and the Flash Generator fires to simulate the gun firing
9 The crew of the tank being attacked see the flash and smoke of the gun firing
10 Laser pulses are picked up by a Detector on the target tank
11 The 'under attack' lamp on the target tank Control Unit is illuminated
12 Communication is established between the Rx/Tx Units of the two tanks, and the true range is measured
13 Taking into account this true range value, the range set into the Control Unit, and the characteristics of the type of ammunition selected, the equipment computes the fall of shot

14 The fall of shot is indicated in the Gunner's Eyepiece Attachment. Suppose that on this occasion it is to the left and low; this is indicated by small red lamps

15 The loader reloads by pressing the load button

16 Another round is deducted from the ammunition stock and the 'loaded' light comes on after the preset delay

17 The gunner re-lays and fires again

18 The equipment performs the functions 8 to 13 above

19 If, this time, the gunner is on target, a 'hit' is indicated in his Eyepiece Attachment by red lamps

20 The Smoke Pyrotechnic on the attacked vehicle is ignited and the 'killed' lamp on its Control Unit is illuminated

21 The Simfire equipment on the killed tank is disabled and the vehicle can take no further part in the exercise

(Simfire also provides a relay that is actuated when a tank is killed and so may be used to cut out tank auxiliaries, radio, etc)

Simfics is a development of Simfire to enable the crew to carry out simulated engagements on a tank fitted with IFCS (Integrated Fire Control System) and the

Above: Simray. An umpire about to use his Simray umpire's gun to 'Kill' a passing Chieftain. The equipment consists of the laser projector, battery and radio pack, antenna and cables, total weight 9.5kg. The gun can be used in various ways during exercises — to check a tank to see it isn't cheating and has its Simfire equipment switched on; to impose casualties when vehicles go out of bounds, over dummy minefields etc; in conjunction with a gun or missile system not equipped with Simfire; to initiate pop-up targets or other visual effects during training. This versatile gun can be used on foot, in a vehicle or a helicopter. / *Solatron Electronic Group*

Tank Laser Sight. It can also be used for the reversionary techniques using known or estimated ranging and the ballistic graticule. Simfire and Simfics are invaluable training aids which maintain a high level of operational awareness among tank crews

The Real Thing

Before leaving the subject of training simulators I must make the point that no amount of simulation, however realistic it may become, can ever entirely take the place of live driving and firing. Without the *real thing* no tank crew can ever be properly trained. However, good simulators, like those I have described, do produce worthwhile results and are now an essential part of the training of Chieftain tank crews.

Postscript:MBT 80

As I was completing this book in mid-September 1978, an announcement was made in the national press, heralding the governmental decision to go ahead with the future main battle tank to replace Chieftain towards the end of the century. Headlines read: 'New all-British tanks to cost £1 million each' (*Daily Telegraph*): '£1,000 million to be spent on new battle tank to replace the Chieftain' (*The Times*); '£1,000,000,000 — just to catch up' (*Sunday Times*). As all these headlines emphasise the monetary angle it is worth while getting the amounts they mention into proper perspective. When Chieftain entered service in 1966/67 it cost approximately double is predecessor Centurion. MBT 80 has been estimated at three times the cost of Chieftain, which if one takes inflation into consideration is not too bad. However, the amount per AFV, discounting development costs, is likely to be about £900,000, so the real question to be answered is will it be worth that sort of money? The *Sunday Times* makes a comparison with the price of the American XM1, which will replace their ageing M60s — its cost was estimated at £275,000 per tank in 1972, it now has escalated to £737,000, not far short of MBT 80.

So what will the British Army get for that sort of money and will it be worth it? A few significant details about MBT 80 have been released, but for obvious security reasons most of them are still classified. The tank will have as its main armament a new British 120mm rifled gun, which I have already mentioned in Chapter 5. This is in preference to the German 120mm smooth bore gun, which was another possible choice. The Americans have agreed to fit the German gun into half their XM1s and both they and the Germans have tried to persuade us to buy the German gun, for the sake of ammunition standardisation within NATO. However, despite the need to standardise whenever possible, I for one support the British decision to go for a rifled gun, as it has a far greater potential for future development than the smooth bore. Among other varieties of ammunition the gun will fire both HESH and APDS types of armour defeating rounds. The latter will probably be an entirely new fin stabilised (FSAPDS) round which is very much more lethal than conventional APDS. The gun control equipment will take advantage of all that has been learnt from IFCS, with all the improvements that this new system brings, while the choice of a three man turret means that we are sticking with a live loader and not following the Russians example of replacing him by an automatic loading system. This is sound commonsense when one considers the 25% reduction in crew endurance which the loss of the loader incurs. Remembering the type of battle ahead of the tanks of 1 British Corps in any future conflict, then the fourth crewman will be worth his weight in gold.

For protection MBT 80 will, like the Shir 2 — which no doubt it is bound to resemble — be fitted with Chobham armour. The XM1 also has Chobham armour and it is anyone's guess as to which other new main battle tanks will also be so equipped. It looks a good deal bulkier than conventional armour but it certainly offers far greater protection, and the designers of MBT 80 hope to keep the all up weight down to about that of Chieftain.

MBT 80 will have a greatly increased performance both in manoeuvrability and speed, with a probable top speed of around 40mph. The engine to produce the necessary power — about 1,500bhp, giving a power to weight ratio of 27 to 1 which is more than double that of Chieftain — has yet to be chosen. The two main contenders are the Rolls-Royce CV12, a proven diesel which I have already described, and a novel American gas turbine from the Aco Lycoming Company, known as the AGT 1500. It is claimed that this engine is quieter, lighter and less likely to give away the tank's position by emitting a lot of tell-tale exhaust smoke. However, gas turbines do consume a lot more fuel, one assessment is a worrying 60% more, so resupply on the battlefield becomes an even greater headache, and they are as yet unproven as tank engines. The Army is delaying any decision for a year whilst trials take place in the USA.

The hull will be built by ROF Leeds, the gun by ROF Nottingham. MVEE have now begun the project definition stage and aim to produce the first prototypes in the early 1980s, with the tank going into service in the 1990s.

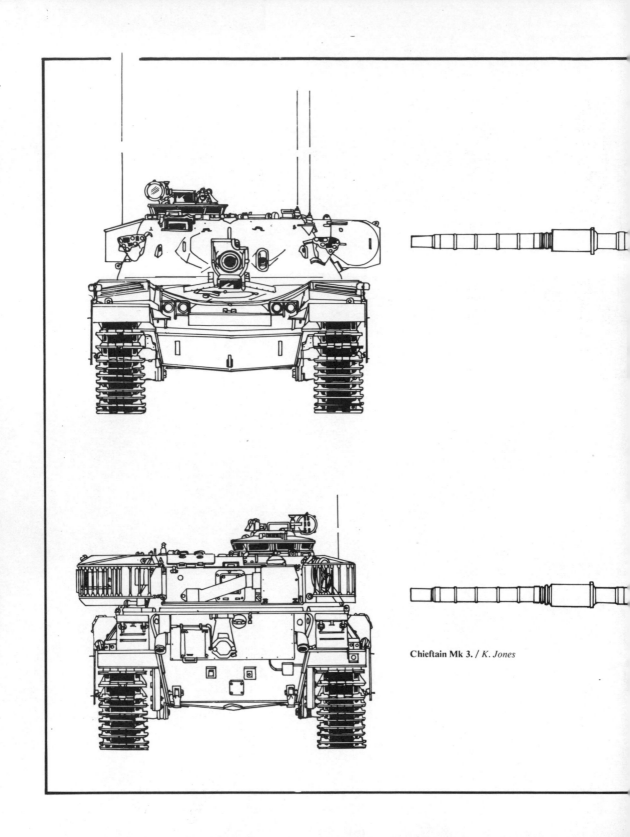

Chieftain Mk 3. / *K. Jones*